Sorrento, Capri & Amalfi Coast

Nick Bruno

Credits

Footprint credits

Editor: Alan Murphy
Production and layout: Jen Haddington
Maps: Gail Townsley

Managing Director: Andy Riddle
Content Director: Patrick Dawson
Publisher: Alan Murphy
Publishing Managers: Felicity Laughton,
Jo Williams, Nicola Gibbs
Marketing and Partnerships Director:
Liz Harper
Marketing Executive: Liz Eyles
Trade Product Manager: Diane McEntee
Account Managers: Paul Bew, Tania Ross
Advertising: Renu Sibal, Elizabeth Taylor
Finance: Phil Walsh

Photography credits
Front cover: Danilo Ascione/Shutterstock
Back cover: Dan Breckwoldt/Shutterstock

Printed in Great Britain by CPI Antony Rowe,
Chippenham, Wiltshire

Every effort has been made to ensure that
the facts in this guidebook are accurate.
However, travellers should still obtain advice
from consulates, airlines, etc about travel
and visa requirements before travelling.
The authors and publishers cannot
accept responsibility for any loss, injury or
inconvenience however caused.

Publishing information
Footprint *Focus Sorrento, Capri & Amalfi Coast*
1st edition
© Footprint Handbooks Ltd
March 2012

ISBN: 978 1 908206 51 0
CIP DATA: A catalogue record for this book is
available from the British Library

® Footprint Handbooks and the Footprint
mark are a registered trademark of Footprint
Handbooks Ltd

Published by Footprints
6 Riverside Court
Lower Bristol Road
Bath BA2 3DZ, UK
T +44 (0)1225 469141
F +44 (0)1225 469461
footprinttravelguides.com

Distributed in the USA by Globe Pequot
Press, Guilford, Connecticut

The content of Footprint *Focus Sorrento,
Capri & Amalfi Coast* has been extracted from
Footprint's *Naples & Amalfi Coast* which was
researched and written by Nick Bruno.

Contents

5 Introduction
    4 *Map: Sorrento, Capri and Amalfi Coast*

6 Planning your trip
    6 Places to visit in Sorrento, Capri and Amalfi Coast
    8 Getting to Sorrento, Capri and Amalfi Coast
    9 Transport in Sorrento, Capri and Amalfi Coast
    12 Where to stay in Sorrento, Capri and Amalfi Coast
    13 Food and drink in Sorrento, Capri and Amalfi Coast
    16 Festivals in Sorrento, Capri and Amalfi Coast
    19 Essentials A-Z

23 Sorrentine Peninsula and Amalfi Coast
    24 Sorrentine Peninsula
    30 Sorrentine Peninsula listings
    34 Amalfi Coast
    41 Amalfi Coast listings
    46 Salerno and Paestum
    50 Salerno and Paestum listings

53 Capri, Ischia and Procida
    54 Capri
    56 *Map: Capri*
    60 Capri listings
    64 Ischia
    67 *Map:* Ischia
    68 Ischia listings
    72 Procida
    74 *Map: Procida*
    75 Procida listings

77 Vesuvius, Herculaneum and Pompeii
    78 Ercolano and Vesuvius
    80 *Map: Herculaneum*
    85 Ercolano and Vesuvius listings
    88 Pompeii and around
    91 *Map: Pompeii*
    96 Pompeii and around listings

99 Footnotes
    100 Index

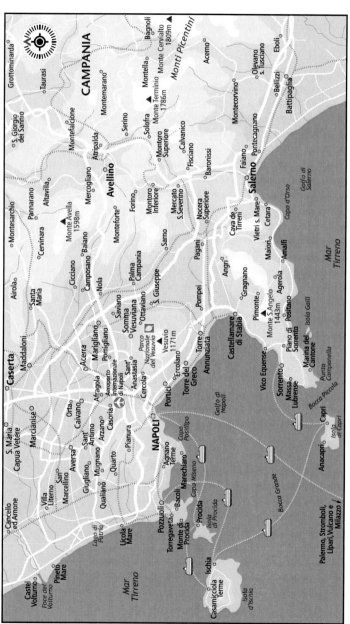

Southeast of anarchic Naples and the fecund but fatal volcano Vesuvius, the Apennine peaks of the Sorrentine Peninsula plunge into the Tyrrhenian Sea. Around Sorrento, along La Costiera Amalfitana to Salerno, unfold limestone cliffs harbouring fishing communities, terraced groves, limpid inlets, castle gardens and majolica-domed churches. The impossibly scenic SS163 'Amalfi Drive' connects villages clinging to the rocks, while puffs of Amalfi's maritime adventures adorn the Byzantine and Arabic-Norman architecture.

Ravello's serene heights inspire composers and artists. On the crater rim of mainland Europe's only active volcano and AD 79 time capsules – Pompeii and Herculaneum – throbs the aftershocks of nature and history. At Paestum, now home of mozzarella balls and roaming buffalo, ancient Greeks colonists built columns that became the climactic vision of Grand Tourists.

Then there are the islands of the Bay of Naples. Capri is all about drama, escapism and the molto chic; Ischia heals with thermal springs, tropical gardens and sandy beaches; while Procida has earthy charm and pastel-painted villages immortalized in the film *Il Postino*. And it's the star of that film, the Neapolitan Massimo Troisi who encapsulates the best of the region's people – the warmth, humour and passion for simple pleasures. Rejoicing in Campania's natural bounty, Epicureanism flourished in its purest philosophical sense in these bays. It survives in Herculaneum's papyrus scrolls and the traditions of the coast's resourceful artisan producers and cooks.

Planning your trip

Places to visit in Sorrento, Capri and Amalfi Coast

Sorrentine Peninsula and Amalfi Coast

Tectonic forces lifted limestone rocks to create these spectacular coastlines. The *Penisola Sorrentina* extends from Roman spa-town Castellammare di Stabia to the wild headland of Punta Campanella, whose glittering splinter, the island of Capri, sits nearby. From Sant'Agata sui Due Golfi, which straddles the gulfs of Naples and Salerno, *la Costiera Amalfitana* and the meandering SS163 Amalfi Drive (beloved of coupé-car advertisers and slow coaches) begins. Soaring cliffs of the Monti Lattari plunge down to an azure sea studded with hidden coves and grottoes – those natural hideouts of pirates and canoodling film stars. Rustic traditions and the tastiest produce thrive amid the terraced olive and citrus groves, campanile-chiming villages and fishing harbours. Pebbly beaches, dramatic ravines and stunning walks like the Trail of the Gods abound. Touristy Sorrento has its charms, especially towards Massa Lubrense. Positano defines the pastel-painted picturesque harbour turned chic resort. Amalfi basks in its glorious maritime past while lofty Ravello's Norman-Saracenic gardens and glorious vistas are a breath of ethereal air. The bedlam of the Second World War may have seized Salerno yet its *lungomare* and Moorish cathedral cloisters make it worth the detour. Towards the untamed Cilento Coast, Graeco-Roman Paestum and its ancient temples emerge like a vision of a lost civilization.

Capri, Ischia and Procida

The three islands of Capri, Ischia and Procida offer their own unique dreams and adventures. Glamour, glitz and the jet-set are synonymous with Capri, the largest and bluest chip off the old Sorrentine Peninsula's limestone rock. So hilly and craggy is Capri that you can easily escape the daily invasion of mass tourism and bask in the island's wild wonders by ducking down a scented lane or by chartering a boat. Emperors Augustus and Tiberius, and writers like Graham Greene and Axel Munthe have all added to its allure as an idyllic retreat of rustic epicurean pleasures and hedonistic japes.

Both Ischia and Procida were plopped into the bay by the Campi Flegrei volcanic caldera. Vestiges of its heated volcanic past can be seen in Ischia's thermal springs, while Procida is made up of four curvy craters that form stunning bays backed by honey-hued tufa rock. Ischia's 46 sq km contain a dead volcano – Monte Epomeo – subtropical gardens and beaches of volcanic sand fizzing with fumaroles. Tiny Procida is all about intimacy, earthiness and relaxation – its leafy lanes lead to pastel-coloured fishing villages and beaches.

Vesuvius, Herculaneum and Pompeii

Below Vesuvius, compelling time capsules of Roman life continue to astonish archaeologists and visitors. This is *La Zona Rossa*, the Red Zone, the area that will feel the true force of mainland Europe's only active volcano one day. For a heart-pounding dose of humble pie, take a walk around the crater rim of Vesuvius and peer into its depths. There are incredible walks in the Parco Nazionale di Vesuvio and time-travel explorations at Pompeii, Ercolano, Oplontis, Boscoreale and Stabiae. Combine a walk around the

Best of Sorrento, Capri and Amalfi Coast

Baia di Ieranto and Marina del Cantone Towards wild Punta Campanella are the emerald and azure waters of the Bay of Ieranto and nearby Marina del Cantone, where yachts drop anchor, snorkellers and swimmers splash around and diners eat fresh seafood at beachside restaurants on stilts. Page 28.

Sentiero degli Dei The Trail of the Gods consists of two trails (a lower trail and a higher ridge walk) and is best tackled going westwards, for backpack-dropping views of Capri and the Amalfi Coast – it reaches the most divine heights between Grotta Biscotto and Nocella. Page 28.

Ravello Splendidly isolated and refined Ravello has inspired literary works and epic operas, including Wagner's *Parsifal*. Its lofty location and genteel atmosphere is the backdrop to the annual, highbrow cultural scrum, the Ravello Festival, but its real charm lies in its Norman-Saracenic villas with their magical garden terraces and shimmering coastal views, and an alluring Romanesque Duomo. Page 38.

Paestum Mainland Italy's most important Greek ruins and its three impressive Doric temples emerge out of the wild meadows on the plains of the Sele River – a vision of a lost civilization. Arty adventurers like Shelley, Canova and Goethe made it the climax of the Grand Tour. Page 47.

Monte Solaro As you rise serenely to the 600-m zenith of Capri on a single-seat chairlift, your feet dangle above terraced gardens and Anacapri's chiming bells fade into the distance. On top, you can only linger, enjoying an ice cream and surveying shimmering vistas of the Faraglioni Rocks and the bays of Naples and Salerno. Page 58.

Vesuvius Mainland Europe's only active volcano may not have erupted since 1944 but don't underestimate 'Il Dominatore'. Vulcanologists reckon there's 400 sq km of molten rock 8 km below its fizzing fumaroles. A summit trip to allows you to peer into its crater and down old lava fields to Pompeii and across the bay. Page 78.

Herculaneum The compact well-to-do Roman resort buried by over 15 m of pyroclastic debris by the AD 79 eruption reveals fine architectural details and artistic riches that allow you to imagine the cultured beachside lifestyle of its doomed inhabitants. Page 79.

Pompeii Nothing prepares you for the scale of the best-known archaeological dig of them all – a town buried in a searing volcanic time capsule for nearly 2000 years. Amid its villas and public spaces, filled with mosaics, frescoes and Latin graffiti, captivating insights into Roman life are still coming to light. Page 88.

ancient well-heeled beachside resort of Herculaneum, where skeletons, jewels and the Villa dei Papiri's priceless library of scrolls are still coming to light, with a journey around mind-blowing Pompeii. Along the *Miglio d'Oro* (the Golden Mile) there are dozens of 18th-century, Bourbon-era *Ville Vesuviane*. Vesuvian soil yields the tastiest produce including San Marzano tomatoes, apricots, artichokes, persimmons, and grapes that produce the white Vesuvio DOC and Lacryma Christi wines.

Getting to Sorrento, Capri and Amalfi Coast

Air

From UK and Ireland Flying to Naples International Airport (Aeroporto Internazionale di Napoli, also known as Aeroporto Capodichino) is the most convenient option as it's within easy reach of the city and other attractions. Year-round direct flights leave from Dublin, London Heathrow, London Gatwick and London Stansted airports. The main airlines providing year-round direct flights are **Alitalia**, **Aerlingus**, **British Airways** and **easyJet**. Some carriers like **Thomson** run charter flights in the spring and summer months from London and other UK airports including Belfast, Birmingham, Bristol, East Midlands, Glasgow, Manchester and Newcastle. Edinburgh and Liverpool are served by **easyJet** from April to October.

From North America There are no year-round direct flights to Naples from North America. Rome Fiumincino is the nearest airport you can fly direct to, with **Alitalia** and **Delta** flights from New York and Toronto. **Alitalia**, **Air Canada**, **Air France**, **British Airways**, **Delta** and **KLM** also fly to large Italian airports Milan Malpensa and Venice Marco Polo. London, Munich and Paris are other possible hubs with lots of connecting flights to Naples.

From rest of Europe There are direct flights to Naples from many European cities including Amsterdam, Athens, Barcelona, Basel, Berlin, Brussels, Bucharest, Frankfurt, Geneva, Hanover, Kiev, Madrid, Monaco, Munich, Paris, Prague, Stockholm, Stuttgart, Vienna and Zurich. Carriers include **Aerosvit**, **Air One**, **Air France**, **Alitalia**, **Brussels Airlines**, **easyJet**, **Clickair**, **Iberia**, **Lufthansa**, **Meridiana**, **Tuifly**, **Vueling** and **Sky Europe**.

Airport information

Naples International Airport ① *NAP, T081-751 5471/081-789 6259, gesac.it*, also known as Capodichino Airport, is situated about 7 km northeast of the centre of Naples. Recent additions to the airport complex have not drastically changed its feel as a small airport of a manageable size. Buses to central Naples are fairly reliable – they all stop at the main train station, Napoli Centrale, and many drop passengers near the port – so connections with other transport services are usually straightforward. In the Arrivals hall there's an EPT (local tourist board) desk where you can find out tourist information and buy the Artecard, and car hire desks including **Avis** ① *T081-780 5790, avis.co.uk*, **Europcar** ① *T081-780 5643, europcar.co.uk*, and **Hertz** ① *T081-780 2971, hertz.co.uk*.

Airport transfer options

There are countless ways to reach each resort. You could travel in style with a reputable private chauffeur such as **Benvenuto Limos** ① *T346-684 0226, benvenutolimos.com*. Alternatively, **Curreri Viaggi** ① *T081-801 5420, curreriviaggi.it, services 0900-1930, €10 one way*, runs infrequent buses to and from Pompeii and along the Sorrentine peninsula. The journey to Sorrento takes 75 minutes. Otherwise, less-direct routes involve taking the ANM Alibus or a taxi to Naples (see below), the region's transport hub for Circumvesuviana rail, mainline rail (for Salerno) and seaborne services along the coast or to the islands (see Sea section, page 12).

    The **Alibus** runs every 30 minutes from 0630 to 2330 between the airport, piazza Garibaldi (20 mins) and the port terminal at piazza Municipio (35 mins). Tickets cost €3 and can be bought on board: they are valid for 90 minutes and can be used on public transport. If you opt for a **taxi**, you are plunged into Neapolitan chaos at the taxi rank outside Arrivals. Make sure you get an authorized cab (most are white and should have a laminated card with tariff list on the back seat) and either agree to a *prezzo fisso* (fixed price: a journey to central Naples is around €30) or that the *tassista* (taxi driver) puts on his *tassimetro* (metre).

Rail

There are no direct rail links to Naples from the UK. However there are train services to Milan, Turin, Venice, Padua and Verona from European cities, including Paris, Munich, Vienna and Geneva; you can then use **Trenitalia** (trenitalia.com) trains to reach Naples. Travel by rail from the UK involves taking the **Eurostar** (eurostar.com) service from London St Pancras to Paris Gare du Nord (2 hrs 25 mins) and then crossing Paris to the Gare de Bercy to catch a direct overnight sleeper to Milan or Venice Santa Lucia in northern Italy, from where you can catch a train to Naples which takes another six hours. Daytime travel is also possible but you'll have to spend a night in either Paris, Milan or Geneva. Another alternative is an overnight train from Paris Bercy to Roma Termini, which takes 18 hours. Buy tickets through **Rail Europe** ① *T0844 848 4064, raileurope.co.uk, raileurope.com*, or **SNCF** (voyages-sncf.com). For comprehensive information on rail travel throughout Europe, consult seat61.com.

Road

Car If you're up for the 2000-km journey and can afford the petrol, you could drive from the UK to Naples in a leisurely 30 hours (if you're lucky) – a few overnight stops on the way would make for a more pleasant adventure. The classic route from the UK is through France, entering Italy through the Mont Blanc tunnel where you will arrive in the gorgeous Italian Alps, just north of Turin. Italian *autostrade* take you down to Naples; perhaps choose a route to take in towns and sights on the way. Having a car is a bonus if you want to explore Campania but it's more of hindrance for those based in Naples itself as Neapolitan traffic can be a frightening prospect, especially for the uninitiated. Car theft and parking is also a big problem in the city so think thrice before opting to drive in Naples.

Bus/coach Eurolines ① *T041-538 2118, eurolines.com*, run long-distance coaches across Europe. The tortuous journey from London to Naples takes about 36 hours, stopping at Paris and Milan on the way.

Sea

Naples is very much on the Mediterranean cruise liner route. Colossal ships dock around the impressive Fascist-era **Stazione Marittima** ① *T081-551 4448, terminalnapoli.it*, terminal building on the Molo Angioino. A good place to research into the pros and cons of cruise holidays and operators is cruises.co.uk, which contains a wealth of reviews.

Transport in Sorrento, Capri and Amalfi Coast

Rail

Italy's hugely extensive, efficient and affordable rail network is the best way to get around the country. It is served by air-conditioned and splendid Eurostar Italia trains (ES); direct and convenient InterCity trains (IC); and the slightly less regular Regionale (REG) and

Interregionale (IR) trains, both of which stop at many more stations. All can be booked at trenitalia.com; booking is advised for Eurostar Italia and InterCity services. **Trenitalia** ① *T89-20-21 from within Italy, T+39 0668-475475 from outside Italy, trenitalia.com*, has details of all routes, service issues and latest discount offers.

The **Napoli Centrale** station is on crazy, traffic-ridden piazza Garibaldi. Be especially careful in and around the crowded station, keeping a close eye on your valuables and your wallet, as its frenzied and humid environment can be disorientating and the area is frequented by some dodgy characters and pickpocket squads. The main train line runs north to Rome and south to Salerno and Calabria.

Local railways The **Ferrovia Circumvesuviana** (T800-053939, vesuviana.it) runs between Naples (Stazione Circumvesuviana, just off piazza Garibaldi) and the satellite towns east of the city, below Vesuvius (including Ercolano and Pompei) and along the Sorrentine Peninsula as far as Sorrento. It's a reliable service and cheap to use, although overcrowded at peak times.

Road

Car Having your own vehicle is more of a burden than a bonus in Naples as the traffic is horrendous and car crime is rife. Put it this way – running a car in this city demands some of the highest insurance premiums on the planet! However, if you plan to brave the roads and tour Campania's mountainous interior, having your own transport will allow you to visit more rural destinations that are difficult to reach by bus or train. For those heading into the city and the islands, the most convenient and central car park is **Parcheggio Buono Molo Beverello** ① *piazza Municipio, T335-499658, parcheggiobeverello.com, daily 0600-2100*, which is next to the Molo Beverello port.

EU nationals taking their own car into Italy need to have an International Insurance Certificate (also known as a *Carta Verde*) and a valid national or EU licence. Those holding a non-EU licence need to take an International Driving Permit with them.

Speed limits are 130 kph on *autostrade* (motorways), 110 kph on dual carriageways and 50 kph in towns. (Limits are 20 kph lower on motorways and dual carriageways when the road is wet.) The **A1** links Rome and Naples, passing Capua and Caserta and through the northern suburbs before it becomes the **A3**, which runs eastwards below Vesuvius and towards Salerno. Approaching the city, vehicles use the **Tangenziale di Napoli**, a huge ring road on stilts that sweeps westwards above the city. It has various exits and can be a tad confusing and overwhelming for those not used to the fluid Neapolitan traffic – Uscita 1 (Exit 1) on the Tangenziale is for Capodichino and Naples International airport. For those staying north or west of the city at Capodimonte, Vomero, Fuorigrotta or the Campi Flegrei, it's best to use the Tangenziale to avoid the city's traffic mayhem downtown. Drivers heading to the port or east of the city towards Ercolano, the Sorrentine Peninsula and Amalfi Coast should continue to the intersection near San Giovanni a Teduccio, where the A3 starts. *Autostrade* are toll roads, so keep cash in the car as a back-up even though you can use credit cards on the blue 'viacard' gates. **Autostrade** ① *T055-420 3200, autostrade. it*, provides information on motorways in Italy and **Automobile Club d'Italia** ① *T06-49981, aci.it*, provides general driving information. It also offers roadside assistance with English-speaking operators on T116.

If you intend to drive in the Apennine and Lattari mountains along the Amalfi Coast, take extra care, certainly in winter due to the icy conditions but also in summer when there are a lot of cyclists on the road. The winding Amalfi Drive (SS163) is particularly taxing in the summer, when its narrow hairpins are clogged with holiday traffic and coaches. Wet conditions combined with often-oily, poorly maintained roads throughout the region make for treacherous driving conditions, requiring care.

Be aware that there are restrictions on driving in historic city centres, indicated by signs with black letters ZTL (*zona a traffico limitato*) on a yellow background. If you ignore these signs, you are liable for a fine. Parking is usually available outside the *centro storico* for €2-5 an hour depending on the location. City hotels will either provide parking for guests or be able to direct you to the nearest car park.

Since July 2007 on-the-spot fines for minor traffic offences have been in operation; typically they range from €150 to €250 (always get a receipt). Note the following legal requirements: the use of mobile telephones while driving is not permitted; front and rear seatbelts must be worn, if fitted; children under 1.5 m may only travel in the back of the car. Italy has very strict laws on drink driving: the legal limit is 0.5 g per litre of blood compared to the UK's 0.8 g). If your car breaks down on the carriageway, you must display an emergency triangle and wear a reflective jacket in poor visibility. Car hire companies should provide both of these but check the boot when you pick up your car.

Car hire Car hire is available at Naples airport. You are advised to book your hire car before you arrive in the country, especially at busy times of year. Car hire comparison websites and agents are a good place to start a search for the best deals: try carrentals.co.uk, avis. com, europcar.co.uk and hertz.co.uk. Check what each hire company requires from you: some companies will ask for an International Driving Licence alongside your normal driving licence; others are content with an EU licence. You will also need a credit card, so, if you book ahead, make sure that the named credit card holder is the same as the person renting and driving the car. Most companies have a lower age limit of 21 years, with a young driver surcharge for those under 25, and require that you've held your licence for at least a year. Confirm the company's insurance and damage waiver policies and keep all your documents with you when you drive.

Bicycle If your thighs are up to it and you are confident on roads populated with fast and crazy drivers, cycling around the rural areas of Campania can be memorable. Arm yourself with a good map: Edizioni Multigraphic and Touring Club Italiano do excellent road maps and Kompass cater for outdoor enthusiasts seeking wilder climbs. Bikes are allowed on many train services: check out trenitalia.com for more information. Bike hire is available at **Rent a Bike Italy** ① *T346-847 1141, rentalbikeitaly.com*, and **Napoli Bike** ① *Riviera di Chiaia, T081-411 934, napolibike.com*. The former can also arrange guided excursions on the Amalfi Coast and epic climbs up Vesuvius. The **European Cycling Federation** (ecf.com) promotes cycling in Europe and has some good advice as well as links to companies that provide biking tours in the region.

Bus/coach With trains so fast, cheap and efficient, it is only in the more rural areas that buses provide a useful service. Check with the local tourist information office to confirm times and pick-up points, as well as to find out where to buy tickets (it's often a nearby newsagent or tobacconist). Travelling around cities by bus is easier as these services are regular. Again you can buy tickets from newsagents, tobacconists (look for a big T sign) and even some cafés: if you intend to make a number of journeys, buy a stash of tickets or a travel card such as Unico Campania, Unico Costiera or Unico Ischia (a day's unlimited travel for under €5). Always remember to validate your ticket when you board by stamping it in the machine onboard. The main bus companies in the region are **ANM** (anm.it), which runs buses around Naples and the suburbs, while **SITA** (sitabus.it) and **Eavbus** (eavbus.it) provide regional services.

Sea

There are many operators who provide maritime passenger services to and from the islands (Capri, Ischia and Procida), along the Sorrentine Peninsula (including Sorrento) and along the Amalfi Coast (Amalfi and Positano) towards Salerno. The port terminal (opened in 2008) at **Calata Porta di Massa**, off via Cristoforo Colombo, now handles the bulk of the ferry (*navi/ traghetti*) services, whereas nearby **Porto Beverello**, near piazza Municipio, is the place to go for the swifter hydrofoils (*aliscafi*) and catamarans (*catamarani*). The smaller and less hectic quayside at **Mergellina** now handles the bulk of the faster and more comfortable *aliscafi* services (hydrofoils) to Ischia. In the summer especially, the most comfortable way of reaching Positano, Amalfi and Minori is to take a hydrofoil from the port of Napoli Beverello. Further west in the Campi Flegrei at the port of **Pozzuoli** there are services to and from Ischia (Ischia Porto, Casamicciola and Forio) and Procida (Marina Grande). The main carriers are: **Alilauro** ① *T081-497 2211, alilauro.it,* **Caremar** ① *T081-017 1998, caremar.it,* **Linee Marittime Artenopee** ① *T081-807 1812, consorziolmp.it,* **Medmar** ① *T081-552 2838, medmargroup.it,* **Metro del Mare** ① *T199-600700, metrodelmare.com,* **NLG** ① *Navigazione Libera del Golfo, T081-552 0763, navlib.it,* **Procidalines** ① *T081-896 0328,* **Procidamar** ① *T081-497 2278, procida.net,* and **SNAV** ① *T081-761 2348, snav.it.*

Where to stay in Sorrento, Capri and Amalfi Coast

The **Sorrentine Peninsula**, **Amalfi Coast** and **the islands** are well-established tourist destinations and have lots of choice for most budgets. Majolica tiles and shimmering views are standard at Amalfi's swanky Hotel Santa Caterina and homely Marina Riviera (see page 41), as well as at Ravello's posh Palazzo Sasso (see page 41) and Positano's elegant Le Sireneuse (see page 41). Down at Paestum, the Oleandri Resort (see page 50) resembles a Red Sea hotel. Budget options include Villaggio Nettuno (see page 30) at the Marina di Cantone and a Sant'Agnello hostel with boutique hotel fittings – Seven H (see page 30). On the islands, there are truly magical hotels for those with deep pockets. Capri has the boutique darling J.K. Place (see page 60) while Anacapri's Caesar Augustus (see page 60) was King Farouk of Egypt's favourite retreat. Ischia has a glut of spa hotels (with varying standards of cleanliness) as well as the fabulous yet affordable Albergo Il Monastero (see page 68), housed in a castle convent. Procida's planning laws have resulted in a dearth of decent hotels, with La Vigna (see page 75) a standout choice.

Vesuvius, **Ercolano** and **Pompeii** have less impressive accommodation. However, things are improving and prices are generally much cheaper, except perhaps at Pompeii which has a captive market.

Apartments and agriturismi

For those seeking freedom, whether it's in the city or on the coast, renting an apartment or villa is a great option. A small, family-run outfit such as Amalfi Vacation (amalfivacation.it) can be the easiest to deal with, while large brokers like **Ville in Italia** (villeinitalia.com) and **Cuendet** (cuendet.com) have hundreds of properties to choose from. Rustic *agriturismi* farm stays offer a taste of the rustic life and home-made food. Examples include Bel Vesuvio Inn (see page 85) on the slopes of Vesuvius, and Il Castagno (see page 42)

Price codes

Where to stay

€€€€ over €300   €€€ €200-300

€€ €100-200   € under €100

Prices refer to the cost of two people sharing a double room in the high season.

Restaurants

€€€€ over €40   €€€ €30-40

€€ €20-30   € under €20

Prices refer to the average cost of a two-course meal for one person, including drinks and service charge.

and La Ginestra (see page 30) on the Sorrentine Peninsula – all of which have basic and reasonably priced rooms. The website en.agriturismo-on-line.com is a handy resource for farmstays and apartments.

Food and drink in Sorrento, Capri and Amalfi Coast

Campania is a foodie's heaven. Its fecund volcanic soil and the waters of the Tyrrhenian Sea yield plentiful, tasty and healthy produce and seafood – the term 'Mediterranean diet' was first coined at the University of Salerno. The intense flavours of Campania's vegetables, fruits and seafood need little adornment. It's no coincidence that Graeco-Roman Naples was the natural home of Epicureanism – in its purest philosophical sense – and Bacchanalian revelry.

Neapolitan cuisine

Miseria e nobiltà – poverty and nobility – have shaped *la cucina Napoletana*. While the region's resourceful poor have created two simple world-conquering creations, dried pasta and pizza, 2500 years of foreign influence, especially French and Spanish, with a dash of Arabic, has spawned 'noble' dishes such as *timballi* and *sartù di riso*, as well as rich pastry and ice-cream making traditions.

Massimo di Porzio, vice president of the *Associazione Verace Pizza Napoletana*, is a purist when it comes to pizza making but is always quick to enthuse about the incredible variety in Neapolitan cuisine. Opposite, he recommends 11 classic *piatti napoletani* to try as an introduction to *la gastronomia partenopea*.

Pasticcerie Pastries are world-renowned.

babà a rum-drenched bulbous sponge.

cornetto con crema/con marmellata sweet croissant usually filled with custard or marmalade. A breakfast favourite accompanied by coffee.

pastiera a large tart made with a filling of sweet ricotta and candied fruit.

sfogliatella meaning 'many leaves' or 'layers', *sfogliatelle* are made of thin layers of pastry and filled with ricotta often infused with orange. *sfogliatella riccia* has flaky pastry while *sfogliatella frolla* is the shortcrust version.

struffoli small deep-fried balls of dough covered in honey.

torta caprese chocolate-and-almond cake from Capri.

zeppole Neapolitan doughnuts or fritters, sometimes with cream but always crusted with sugar and served warm.

Coffee In Naples *caffè* is extra strong with a pre-sugared kick to complete the rush it gives. The barista may ask you *'già zuccherato?'* before he makes your caffeine hit, so ask for *'amaro'* (bitter) if you are sweet enough. A glass of water is served to clear your palate.

espresso/normale/un caffè a standard espresso – a double is a *doppio*.

ristretto an even stronger espresso made with less water.

caffè corretto espresso 'corrected' with a shot of alcohol, usually grappa.

macchiato espresso 'marked' or 'stained' with foamy milk on top.

caffè Americano or *lungo* espresso made or served with more hot water.

caffè shakerato iced espresso given the cocktail-shaker treatment.

cappuccino a frothy milky coffee seldom drunk after midday.

latte macchiato/*caffè latte* steamed milk 'marked' or 'stained' with a tiny shot of espresso.

caffè latte shakerato ice-cold *caffé latte* shaken.

Eleven classic Campanian dishes Chosen by Massimo di Porzio, Ristorante-Pizzeria Umberto, Chiaia, Napoli.

ragù di carne alla Genovese Not from Genova but invented by the Genovese family. Small pieces of beef cooked with onions and served with smooth and long tubular *pasta liscia* like *mezzanelli*.

spaghetti alle vongole The classic summer dish is often served with the freshest Vesuvian tomatoes combined with clams. Often called *vermicelli alle vongole*.

baccalà alla Napoletana Preserved cod fried and cooked with tomatoes and onions.

polipetti affogati/polipetti con pomodori Octopus cooked *in bianco* (stewed in its own juices) with wine and black olives, or cooked with tomatoes.

frittura di pesce Medley of lightly fried seafood served with a wedge of lemon.

mozzarella in carozza Mozzarella goes gooey in its fried bread 'carriage'.

parmigiana di melanzane Layers of fried aubergine slices, mozzarella, parmesan, basil and *passata di pomodoro*.

zucchini alla scapece Thin courgette slices marinated in garlic, vinegar and mint (side dish).

zuppa di soffritto di maiale A hearty soup of pig offal, tomatoes and chilli.

sartù di riso/timpano di maccheroni A tasty *ragù* sauce is poured over a mound of rice that contains pieces of *polpettine* (meat balls), aubergine, peas, sausage meat and sometimes provola cheese, then it's baked. There's an *in bianco* (literally white) version without the *ragù* sauce. It often takes the form of a *ciambellone* (large ring). On the same lines is the *timballo o timpano di maccheroni*, a 19th-century dish that consists of a mound of macaroni (a timbale mould resembling a kettle drum is used, hence the name) mixed with layers of filling typically including meaty *ragù*, *salsicciotto piccante* (spicy sausage), hard-boiled egg, tomato salsa and sometimes even brains. It's covered in *pasta frolla* (pastry).

bucatini alla Siciliana Long pasta tubes popular in Naples that are typically served with a rich sauce consisting of aubergine, meatballs, plus *ragù napoletano*, fried mushrooms, parmigiano and mozzarella. It's covered with more meaty *ragù* and baked in an oven.

Culinary treasures of the Amalfi Coast

· Cetara's salted anchovy sauce, *la colatura*, resembles the ancient Roman garum.

· At Gragnano, dried pasta-making was turned into a mass-production industry. In 1860 there were over 80 pasta factories there.

- Minori is famous for 'ndunderi, which resemble ancient Roman *gnocchi* (dumplings).
- At the marine nature reserve of Punta Campanella, hand-woven baskets (*nasse*) are used by local fishermen from April to September to catch *parapandolo*, small rare shrimp famed for their sweet, flavoursome meat.
- The Monti Lattari (Milky Mountains) are named after their dairy products, which have been highly sought after since the days of the Dukes of Amalfi. The pastures of Tramonti, Scala and Agerola produce quality cheeses such as *Provolone di Monaco*, mozzarella, *caciocavallo* and *fior di latte*.

When and where to eat

Breakfast (*colazione*) in Campania may include a caffè latte and/or an espresso accompanied by a pastry, usually a horn-shaped *cornetto* with fillings – *alla crema* (pastry cream), *al cioccolato* (chocolate) or *alla marmellata* (marmalade). On holiday and Sundays locals enjoy a long lunch (*pranzo*), perhaps followed by a cheeky siesta at the height of summer. An *aperitivo* is taken in the early evening, usually in a bar, and is served with *stuzzichini* (nibbles). Restaurants tend to serve lunch 1200-1530 and dinner (*cena*) 1900-2300. Traditionally *un ristorante* was posher than *una trattoria*, which in turn was generally more sophisticated than *un'osteria*, which was once just a rustic inn serving wine and simple dishes; however the distinction between each is blurred these days so the title is not a good indicator of quality, price or ambience.

Campania is one of the cheapest regions to eat out and standards are generally excellent. There are wonderful seafood restaurants in magical places and superb-value *pizzerie* are commonplace. The cornucopia of *contorni* (side dishes) on Campanian menus is a great help for vegetarians.

Wines of Campania

Where once the Campania region was known for the quantity of richly coloured, alcohol-heavy wine produced, it is now creating quality wines with elegance and subtlety. Here are the best of Campania's DOC wines:

Aglianico del Taburno Rosso The Aglianico grape, cultivated in the Benevento province, is aged for two years; its bold taste goes well with cheese.

Campi Flegrei Falanghina Grown in the volcanic soil, the white Falanghina grape has a lightly aromatic bouquet with fruity notes. Goes well with seafood, especially mussels and crustaceans.

Capri Bianco A small, highly prized production of white wine mixing Falanghina, Greco and Biancolella grape varities. Best drunk young, its fresh, dry taste is a perfect match for seafood and cheeses like caciocavallo.

Costa d'Amalfi Bianco Falanghina and Biancolella vines grown on the terraces around Ravello, Furore and Tramonti produce a subtle wine that marries well with light seafood dishes and fresh cheeses. *Rosato* and *rosso* versions are also produced.

Fiano di Avellino A venerable white produced in the Avellino province with floral and hazelnut aromas. Goes well with fish and young cheeses.

Greco di Tufo Probably the best-known DOC along with Fiano. The Greco vine is grown in the Irpinia area, whose volcanic soil gives the wine a rich flavour and good acidity. It works well with Neapolitan seafood dishes, artichokes, rice dishes and soups.

Ischia Bianco Generally a mix of Forastera and Biancolella grapes, it has an intense yellow colour, subtle aromas and is a perfect accompaniment to delicate dishes and light antipasti. There is a sparkling *spumante* version.

Ischia Piedirosso The Piedirosso vine's reddish stalks resemble doves' feet, hence the name. With an aroma of violets, and a little tannic, it goes well with *coniglio all'ischiatana* (Ischian-style rabbit).

Taurasi Rosso Wine from the Aglianico vine grown in the Avellino province is aged for three years in barrels, giving it complex flavours and aromas; perfect for meat dishes and cheeses.

Vesuvio Lacryma Christi Bianco The white Coda di Volpe grape grown on the slopes of Vesuvius is blended with Falanghina and Greco varities. *Rosso*, *rosato* and *spumante* versions are also produced.

Festivals in Sorrento, Capri and Amalfi Coast

Catholic festivals, many with pagan origins and hundreds celebrating saints' days, dominate the calendar. Neapolitans certainly know how to party and display emotion so expect full-on fireworks, food, processions and histrionics. Traditional events celebrate the bounty of land and sea, while an eclectic array of cultural and music extravaganzas entertain locals and visitors across the region.

January

Capodanno (New Year) Concerts and fireworks in many towns and general mayhem all over. Positano sees in the New Year with the **Sagra della Zeppola**, which involves lots of fried pastries (*zeppole*) and festivities.

Festa Nazionale della Befana (6th) Epiphany is celebrated in Italy with Italian children receiving more presents from *la Befana*, a good witch who leaves treats for the good kids and a lump of coal (now some honeycomb candy died black) for naughty ones.

February

Carnevale (14 days before Ash Wednesday) The 'farewell to meat' festival is an excuse for excess that starts a fortnight before Ash Wednesday when Lent begins. All over Campania there are float parades, feasts and flamboyant shows throughout. Paestum puts on a particularly full-on show with masked revellers.

March

Festa Tradizionale dell'Annunziata (24-25th) Paestum's feast day sees market stalls in the *centro storico* showcasing the area's bountiful produce and a procession led by an 18th-century statue of the Madonna.

Settimana della Cultura (late March) The national week of culture allows visitors to take advantage of free museum entrance, special guided tours and cultural events.

April

Easter *Pasqua* (Easter) is celebrated with processions and ceremonies, some dating from the Middle Ages and even pagan times. Celebrations at Sorrento/Massa Lubrense, Sant'Anastasia al Vesuvio and Procida are famously flamboyant, with the scoffing of lots of savoury and sweet pies – *il casatiello* and *la pastiera*.

Processione dei Misteri Statues and contemporary depictions of scenes from the Passion of Christ are taken through the streets of Terra Murata, Procida on Good Friday.

Linea d'Ombra (mid-April) Salerno's film and cultural festival.

May

Festa di San Costanzo (third week of May) Capri's patron saint and protector, who drove away Saracen attacks in the Middle Ages, is honoured with a flower-strewn procession and a host of cultural events.

Maggio dei Monumenti Naples' historic sites can be visited free and some rarely seen sights are opened too. Themed cultural events including lots of concerts and installations in wonderful settings make May a stimulating month to visit.

June

Concerti al Tramonto A season of concerts (June to September), classical and jazz, staged by the San Michele Foundation, custodians of Axel Munthe's enchanting Villa San Michele (sanmichele.org).

Regata Storica delle Quattro Repubbliche Marinare Historic rowing regatta in which the four ancient maritime republics Venice, Amalfi, Genoa and Pisa celebrate their illustrious history with much pomp and ceremony during a week of events culminating in the rowing *palio*. The event, held on the first Sunday in June, rotates between the cities, with Amalfi hosting the celebrations in 2012.

Festa di Sant'Andrea (27th) The statue of Amalfi's patron saint, credited with saving the city by whipping up a storm, is paraded through the streets to commemorate the defeat of Barbarossa's fleet in 1544. On reaching the beach, fishermen return the statue to the Duomo as fast as they can as a mark of their strength and faith. The festival is accompanied by fish in all its forms – fresh and ornamental – music and fireworks.

Estate Amalfitana A summer-long festival of cultural and foodie events including concerts at the Duomo and Grotta dello Smeraldo.

July

Ravello Festival Classical music concerts and other artistic events are staged in spectacular Ravello from July to November (ravellofestival.com).

Festa della Madonna del Carmine (15-16th) On the night before the saint's day, spectacular fireworks light up the Naples sky in a symbolic 'burning' of the campanile of the Chiesa di Madonna del Carmine in piazza Mercato. The following day, mass is celebrated every hour of the day.

Festa di Sant'Anna (26th) Ischia's patron is honoured with a flamboyant procession of crazily adorned floats around the Castello Aragonese amid lots of fireworks (festadisantanna.it).

Festa di San Pantaleone Mass Matinee performances and fireworks celebrate the liquefaction of the saint's blood in Ravello.

August

Ferragosto (15th) Summer bank holiday that heralds an exodus of Italians to the beach.

Sbarco dei Saraceni (14-15th) Saracen raids of the ninth and 10th centuries are marked with spectacular re-enactments and fireworks on the water at Positano.

September

Settembrata Anacaprese Anacapresi come together in late August to early September for themed events and good-natured competition to see which *quartiere* can deliver the finest food, sweetest song and heartiest laugh.

October

Sagra della Castagna All over Campania during the last weekend of October the harvest of sweet chestnuts is celebrated with street parties – at San Cipriano Picentino there's a donkey race (lasagradellacastagna.net).

November

Pane e Olio in Frantoio On the last weekend of November, local producers of extra virgin olive oil and bread promote their goods at numerous tastings across Campania (cittadellolio.it).

Festa di Sant'Andrea (30th) So good is St Andrew that the Amalfitani celebrate their patron saint twice, this time after his *manna* 'miraculously' liquefies, bringing much relief to the populace.

December

Festa di Santa Lucia (13th) St Lucy's day is commemorated in Italy with fire and feasting. At Sorrento's Sagra della Salsiccia e Ceppone, a massive fire is prepared on the 12th, and the following night the feast is celebrated with copious amounts of barbecued sausages and local vino.

Presepi di Natale Naples and Campania are famous for their nativity scenes (*presepi*). Most churches have a tableau replete with Gesù, shepherds and livestock. San Leucio in the province of Caserta has a 'living nativity'.

Essentials A-Z

Customs and immigration
UK and EU citizens do not need a visa but will need a valid passport to enter Italy. A standard tourist visa for those outside the EU is valid for up to 90 days.

Disabled travellers
Italy is beginning to adapt to the needs of disabled travellers but access can still be very difficult due to the age of many historic buildings or the lack of careful planning. For more details and advice, contact a specialist agency before departure, such as **Accessible Italy** (accessibleitaly.com) or **Society for Accessible Travel and Hospitality** (sath.org).

Emergencies
Ambulance T118; **Fire service** T115; **Police** T112 (with English-speaking operators), T113 (*carabinieri*); **Roadside assistance** T116.

Etiquette
Facendo la bella figura (projecting a good image) is important to Italians but down in Campania there is a more laid-back, humorous outlook – the locals are famed for flouting rules and dodging barriers. Neapolitan chattiness is one of the infectious aspects of the region. However, as in the rest of Italy, you should check your change, prices and tariffs. Being *furbo* (sly) and dishonest dealings to gain commercial advantage do not have the same negative connotations in Italy as they do in other cultures. Learn the phrase *non è giusto* (it is not right) as a firm word will be needed from time to time. Unfortunately, *La Dolce Vità Italiana* often leaves a bitter taste.

Take note of public notices about conduct: sitting on steps or eating and drinking in certain historic areas is not allowed. Covering arms and legs is necessary for admission into some churches – in rare cases even shorts are not permitted. Punctuality, like queuing (*facendo la coda*), is an alien concept in Italy, so be prepared to wait on occasion – but not necessarily in line or order.

Families
The family is highly regarded in Italy and children are well treated (not to say indulged), particularly in restaurants (although more expensive restaurants may not admit children). Naples is particularly famed for its family-orientated lifestyle and Neapolitans generally welcome children with open arms. There's plenty to do in Naples and Campania besides endless museum visits: there are seaside attractions aplenty of course, as well as theme parks and a zoo in Fuorigrotta. Note that lone parents or adults accompanying children of a different surname may sometimes need proof of guardianship before taking children in and out of Italy; contact your Italian embassy for the current details on this (Italian embassy in London, T020-7312 2200).

Health
Comprehensive medical insurance is strongly recommended for all travellers to Italy. EU citizens should also apply for a free European Health Insurance Card (ehic.org .uk), which replaced the E111 form and offers reduced-cost medical treatment. Late-night pharmacies are identified by a large green cross outside. Out-of-hours pharmacies are listed in most local newspapers. The accident and emergency department of a hospital is the *pronto soccorso*.

Insurance
Comprehensive travel (and medical) insurance is strongly recommended for

all travellers to Italy. You should check any exclusions, excess and that your policy covers you for all the activities you want to undertake. Keep details of your insurance documents separately. Scanning them, then emailing yourself a copy is a good way to keep the information safe and accessible. Ensure you are fully insured if hiring a car, or, if you're taking your own vehicle, contact your current insurer to check whether you require an international insurance certificate.

Money

The Italian currency is the Euro (€). To change cash or travellers' cheques, look for a *cambio* (exchange office); these tend to give better rates than banks. Banks are open Monday to Friday 0830 to 1300 with some opening again from 1500 to 1600. ATMs that accept major credit and debit cards can be found in every city and town (look around the main piazzas). Many restaurants, shops, museums and art galleries will take major credit cards but paying directly with debit cards is less common than in the UK, so having a ready supply of cash may be the most convenient option. You should also keep some change handy for toll roads if you're driving.

Campania has always been one of Italy's cheapest regions to visit, although chic spots on Capri and along the Amalfi Coast bump up their prices. Not including entrance fees to the sights and transport costs, the cost of a typical day if you're flirting with frugality, is around €60. If you're going to pad out your day with a bit of largesse by eating at some fancier restaurants then we are talking about €120 per person. Expect to pay for the privilege of consuming sitting down in tourist hotspots Positano and Capri.

Opening hours and holidays

Aperto or *chiuso*? It takes getting used to that shops, churches and some sights close for a long lunch. Shutters start coming down around 1230 and don't open until around 1600 onwards, although in busy city and touristy areas most of the sights and some shops stay open. Many places close on a Sunday and/or a Monday (or just the Monday morning). Family-run restaurants or bars may shut for a day during the week. Finally, the Italian holiday month is August. This means that shops, bars, restaurants and even some sights can be closed for a fortnight or longer, especially from 15 August (Ferragosto). They also close for Christmas, New Year and some of January too. August is definitely not the best month to visit Italy.

Police

There are five different police forces in Italy. The *carabinieri* are a branch of the army and wear military-style uniforms with red stripes on their trousers and white sashes. They handle general crime, drug-related crime and public order offences. The *polizia statale* is the national police force, dressed in blue with a thin purple stripe on their trousers. They are responsible for security on the railways and at airports. The *polizia stradale* handles crime and traffic offences on the motorways and drives blue cars with a white stripe. The *vigili urbani* are local police who wear dark blue (in summer) or black (in winter) uniforms with white hats and direct traffic and issue parking fines in the cities. The *guardia di finanza* wears grey uniforms with grey flat hats or green berets (depending on rank). They are charged with combating counterfeiting, tax evasion and fraud.

In the case of an emergency requiring police attention, dial 113 or approach any member of the police or visit a police station (below). If it's a non-emergency, dial 112 for assistance.

Naples: Via Medina 5, T081-551 1190.
Pompeii: Via Sacra 1, T081-856 3511.

Sorrento: Vico Bernardini Rota 14,
T081-807 5311.
Salerno: via Amendola Generale Adalgiso,
T089-613111.
Capri: via Roma 68, T081-837 4211.
Ischia: via Delle Terme, T081-507 4711.
Procida: via Libertà 96, T081-896 0086.

Post

The Italian post service (poste.it) has a not entirely undeserved reputation for unreliablility, particularly when it comes to handling postcards. Overseas post will require *posta prioritaria* (priority mail, which is actually just ordinary mail). You can buy *francobolli* (stamps) at post offices and *tabacchi* (look for T signs). A stamp for a letter or postcard (up to 20g) costs from €0.75 for EU destinations and €1.60 for transatlantic destinations. For letters over 20g and parcels, there is a maze of prices and options.

Safety

Visitors to Naples, its satellites around Vesuvius and Salerno should be most wary. Crowded resorts offer opportunities for criminals on the lookout for valuable items.

Naples has a reputation for petty theft and elaborate street scams which is often exaggerated – unfortunately, the stigma has stuck, which combined with its hectic traffic and general sense of chaos tends to frighten many people away. In reality, random acts of violence are less of a problem here than in many cities around the world. As long as you are extra careful (don't flaunt your wealth and valuables), pickpockets and bag snatchers shouldn't bother you. The use of a money belt to store credit cards, passports and large denominations is advisable – especially when using crowded public transport and visiting chaotic and poor neighbourhoods like Spaccanapoli and the Quartieri Spagnoli. Don't leave bags and valuables unattended in your vehicle, and remove everything from the boot at night. Beware of scams, con artists and sellers of fake goods: if someone offers you electrical goods (camcorders and mobiles are current favourites) or a box of cigarettes on the street, just say *no grazie, non mi interessa* (no thanks, I'm not interested) firmly – and walk on.

Telephone

The dialling codes for the main cities and provinces in Campania are: **Naples** 081; **Salerno** 089; **Caserta** 0823. You need to use these local codes, even when dialling from within the city or region. The prefix for Italy is +39. You no longer need to drop the initial '0' from the area codes when calling from abroad. For directory enquiries call T12.

Time difference

Italy uses Central European Time, GMT+1.

Tipping

It is increasingly common for service to be included in your bill on top of the cover charge. Where this isn't the case (and, sometimes, even when service is included in the bill), tipping is expected wherever there is waiter/waitress service: 50 cents to €1 is fine if you've only had a drink but, for a meal, 10-15% of the total bill is the norm. If you're ordering at the bar, a few spare coins might speed up your coffee and even result in a smile. Taxis may add on extra costs for luggage but an additional tip is always appreciated. Rounding-up prices always goes down well, especially if it means avoiding having to give change – not a favourite Italian habit.

Tourist information

The following official tourist websites are useful places to visit before your trip: inaples.it, amalfitouristoffice.it, capritourism.com, infoischiaprocida.it, turismoinsalerno.it, sorrentotourism.com. If you're travelling by train, also check out trenitalia.it. Once you get to Italy, the regional tourist offices have plenty of leaflets and flyers on local sights and attractions and some offices will also help you to book accommodation.

Combined tickets and travel cards
The region of Campania's various Unico cards offer some free and otherwise discounted entry to many sights, plus savings on public transport. See unicocampania.it.

Voltage
Italy functions on a 220V mains supply. The plugs are the standard European two-pin variety.

Contents

24 Sorrentine Peninsula
    25   Vico Equense
    25   Sorrento
    27   West of Sorrento
    28   Trail of the Gods and other walks
    30   Listings

34 Amalfi Coast
    35   Positano
    35   East of Positano
    37   Amalfi and Atrani
    38   Ravello
    39   Minori, Maiori and Tramonti
    41   Listings

46 Salerno and Paestum
    47   Salerno
    47   Paestum
    50   Listings

Sorrentine Peninsula & Amalfi Coast

Sorrentine Peninsula

As you follow the curves of the SS145 road along the Sorrentine Peninsula, volcanic debris deposited by Vesuvius eventually gives way to the limestone layers of the Apennines that jut into the Mar Tirreno (Tyrrhenian Sea). The first resort you come to is Vico Equense, which survived the worst of the AD 79 eruption and centuries of Saracen attacks, and has an air of faded grandeur in and around its Gothic cathedral and Catalan courtyards. Swooning around Punta Gradelle, you come to the lemon-scented terraces and sheltered *Piano di Sorrento* (Sorrento Plain), whose gentle climate was celebrated by Romans and Romantic artists – it is now popular with package holidaymakers who throng its kitschy streets and luxuriant gardens.

Vico Equense → *For listings, see pages 30-33.*

Vico Equense is probably best known these days as the home of *pizza al metro* (pizza by the metre) at **Da Gigino Università della Pizza** (see page 31). In the 12th century, Carlo I di Angio renamed this former Roman stronghold Aequa and it later became known as Vico Equense (vico from the Latin vicus for village). The Spanish Aragonese continued the rebuilding and today its centre retains elegance in its Gothic cathedral, Catalan courtyards, and some interesting small museums.

Chiesa di Santissima Annunziata
ⓘ *Via Cattedrale, Vico Equense. Daily 0800-1230, 1530-1900, free.*
You wouldn't believe that this peachy clean church sitting above plunging cliffs has 14th-century Gothic origins. As you approach, narrow atmospheric lanes are crammed with Catalan-style buildings from the Aragonese era. An imposing arch cuts through its lofty campanile and draws you into a belvedere area with superb seaward views.

Museo Antiquarium Equano
ⓘ *Casa Municipale, via Filangieri 98, Vico Equense. Mon, Wed and Fri 0900-1300, Tue and Thu 1530-1830, Sat-Sun 0930-1230, free.*
Housed in the town hall is Vico's archaeological museum, whose dusty highlights include fragments left by Etruscans and other Italic tribes as well as Greek remains from the ancient town's necropolis.

Museo Mineralogico Campano
ⓘ *Via San Ciro 2, Vico Equense, T081-801 5668, museomineralogicocampano.it. Mar-Sep Tue-Sat 0900-1300, 1700-2000, Oct-Feb Tue-Sun 0900-1300, 1600-1900, year round Sun and Bank Holidays 0900-1300, €3.*
Mineral-mad Pasquale Discepolo, an engineer and collector, helped open this excellent little Mineralogy Museum of Campania in 1992. It's fascinating if you have just walked around the crater of Vesuvius as some of the crystals created by the volcano can be seen here, including intensely blue lapis lazuli collected on Monte Somma. The museum's palaeontological and anthropological collections include dinosaur fossils and ancient artefacts such as Libyan arrowheads.

Marina di Equa and beaches east of Sorrento
Site of the original ancient settlement Aequana, Marina di Equa has a robust defensive tower, Il Torre di Caporivo, rebuilt in 1608, as well as a long and popular beach lined with parasols and a smattering of restaurants. The beaches at Meta, Seiano and Alimuri are often packed, so it's best to seek out isolated stretches of pebble like Tordigliano, which is accessible by boat.

Sorrento → *For listings, see pages 30-33.*

Suspended 45 m above the sea, Sorrento's cobbled streets and squares combine elegance with lashings of limoncello-kitsch. Roman big shots Augustus and Agrippa sojourned in Surrentum, followed by 19th-century Romantic artists, writers and composers. Ibsen and

Gorky had Sorrentine boltholes, and in 1876 the fresh, lemon-scented Piano di Sorrento air rang with the nihilist rantings of Nietzsche, who famously fell out with Wagner over the composer's religious interpretation of *Parsifal*. Nowadays sunburned Brits form the bulk of the international package-holidaymakers who spill out of the cafés and Disneyland-esque Dotto 'train' on piazza Tasso.

Piazza Tasso, Sorrento

Piazza Tasso, named after the troubled 16th-century poet Torquato Tasso whose statue stands in the centre of the square, is built upon the Graeco-Roman layout of Surrentum. Away from the traffic melee, on via Cesareo, is the **Sedile Dominova**, a 15th-century loggia with *trompe l'œil* frescoes, now a men's social club where old *signori* play cards on wooden tables. Nearby, on corso Italia, is the **Chiesa di Santa Maria del Carmine** with its Baroque stucco work and bright yellow façade.

To the south of piazza Tasso is the unexpected and rather magical sight of the inaccessible **Vallone dei Mulini** (Valley of the Mills), where the ruins of an abandoned watermill have been left to crumble in a deep, dank ravine whose microclimate supports rare ferns. For a hands-on feel of this coastline's early industrial past, you can visit various mills near Amalfi (see page 29).

Heading east from piazza Tasso towards the cathedral, there are some fine medieval palazzos to admire on via Santa Maria della Pietà: **Palazzo Veniero** (No 14) is 13th century, showing Byzantine and Arabic influences, while **Palazzo Correale** (No 24) has a handsome portal, windows and tiled courtyard.

Duomo di San Filippo e San Giacomo

ⓘ *Corso Italia 1, Sorrento, T081-878 2248. Daily 0800-1200, 1600-2000, free.*

The façade of Sorrento's Romanesque cathedral is a tad underwhelming at first glance but look carefully and you'll notice two Roman columns and a majolica-tiled clock face. Inside there's lots of multicoloured marble and naturalistic motifs at the altar, some fine 18th-century Neapolitan School paintings and striking inlaid-wood stalls.

Chiesa di San Francesco d'Assisi

ⓘ *Piazza Francesco Saverio Gargiulo, Sorrento. Daily 0800-1300, 1400-1900, free.*

Heading westwards towards the sea is a must-see religious sight and another panoramic garden terrace. Birdsong and bougainvillea twitter and tumble around the interlaced Arabic arches of the evocative 14th-century monastery cloisters next to the Church of San Francesco. Look out for some fascinating architectural fragments taken from ancient temples. Art exhibitions and classical concerts are held in these incredibly atmospheric surroundings, and there are two 18th-century frescoes in the Baroque church, depicting Sant'Antonio of Padova and San Giacomo. More fabulous sea views can be enjoyed from the Villa Comunale Gardens nearby.

Museo Bottega della Tarsia Lignea

ⓘ *Palazzo Pomarici Santomasi, via San Nicola 28, Sorrento, T081-877 1942, alessandrofiorentinocollection.it. Apr-Oct 0930-1300, 1600-2000, Nov-Mar 0930-1300, 1500-1900, closed Mon and certain public holidays, €8 (includes conducted tour). From corso Italia take via Tasso to via San Nicola.*

Sorrento is famous for its *intarsia* (marquetry) and the town's shops are crammed with traditional inlaid-wood products. Find out more about the history and art of marquetry at this gem of a museum, the Intarsia Museum and Craft Shop, where fine examples of inlaid furniture and objects crafted by the great Sorrento inlayers of the past and their modern counterparts are housed in an elegant 18th-century villa. Exquisite marquetry objects for the home are sold in the shop here.

Museo Correale
ⓘ *Via Correale 50, Sorrento, T081-878 1846, museocorreale.com. Wed-Mon 0900-1330, €8.*
Via Correale has some fine aristocratic residences including the former home of the Correale di Terranova family, which provides a look at the tastes and sumptuous furnishings of the Neapolitan nobility. Its 23 rooms are filled with collections of Greek and Roman marble statuary, early photographic equipment, landscape paintings of the Posillipo School, nativity scene figurines, period costumes and dainty porcelain pieces.

Sunbathing and swimming in Sorrento
Marina Piccola is busy with ferry traffic and backed by sheer cliff walls topped by hotels. **Marina Grande** (despite its name) has more of an intimate, fishing village feel and a pebbly beach strewn with boats. All along here are spindly wooden jetties crammed with sun worshippers and bathers in the summer. There are plenty of other small stony beaches nearby (to the east are **Sant'Agnello** and the **Marinella** beaches; to the west is **Marina di Puolo**) but the most beautiful spots are towards the wilds of **Punta della Campanella**. Some 3 km west of Corso Italia is rocky **Punta del Capo** and a steep-sided pool known as Bagno della Regina Giovanna, which sits beside the ruins of what some claim to be Pollius Felix's Roman villa.

West of Sorrento

Massa Lubrense
The pace of life slows west of Sorrento. Minor roads wind down from the busy SS145 to small picturesque harbours. Towards the rocky end of the peninsula, Punta della Campanella, there are wild walks on old mule tracks with views of Capri, just 5 km away. The **Area Marina Protetta di Punta Campanella** has pristine waters and marine caves like Grotta della Cala di Mitigliano and the Grotta dell'Isca which are ideal for snorkelling.

Located just 5 km west of Sorrento along the peninsula, the town that gives its name to this rocky region is a good base for the adventurous and outdoorsy. Massa Lubrense's original cathedral, **Santissima Annunziata**, has Baroque stucco work and an adjoining Franciscan monastery built in the 1580s. After the havoc wrought by Saracen and Turkish pirates Massa built a new cathedral (redone in the 18th century), **Santa Maria delle Grazie**, which is worth a visit for its majolica flooring and *terrazza* sea views. A steep, meandering lane trails between the houses of old Massa Lubrense to reach the cylindrical tower and battlements of a 14th-century **Aragonese castle**, from where there are dramatic glimpses of Capri.

Marina della Lobra
This intimate little harbour filled with colourful fishing vessels and pleasure boats is just down the road from Massa Lubrense. Amid the higgledy-piggledy buildings is the cheerful *giallo-verde* (yellow-and-green) cupola of the monastery-church of Santa Maria della Lobra (1528), which contains a vaulted ceiling and majolica flooring.

Sant'Agata sui Due Golfi and Torca

Just off the SS145 is the village of Sant'Agata ('on the two Gulfs'), which sits in a commanding position overlooking the two coastlines and bays of Naples and Salerno. Its sights include the Chiesa di Santa Maria delle Grazie, which has an exquisite 17th-century marble, lapis lazuli and mother-of-pearl Florentine altar and a majolica clock face. A minor road accesses the once thriving fishing village of **Torca** at 350 m, where there are incredible views towards Li Galli and the shimmering sea beyond. Pop into one of Torca's three shops (including two *salumerie*) for picnic supplies and a chinwag with friendly shopkeepers and passing maritime characters.

Fiordo di Crappola

This mini fjord hewn out of the rock and its tranquil pebbly beach was a favourite hideout of pirates. It's about a 45-minute walk away from Sant'Agata or else accessible by boat. Where there was once a Greek temple to Apollo there now stands the tiny chapel of San Pietro.

Nerano, Baia di Ieranto and Marina del Cantone

Perched on a ridge at 166 m, the small village of Nerano is the gateway to the idyllic emerald and azure waters of the Bay of Ieranto and nearby Marina del Cantone, where yachts drop anchor and film stars are spotted going for a dip and mixing with locals at seafood restaurants on stilts.

Deserto

Also near Sant'Agata, towards Massa Lubrense, is the religious complex of Deserto, which at 457 m affords 360-degree views across Campania, making it one of the most spectacular spots in Southern Italy. The monastery here was built by Carmelite nuns on the site of a hermitage. Remains of a Greek necropolis found here has led some people to claim that this was the site of an ancient Temple of the Sirens. An inscription on one of the towers reads 'Tempus breve est' ('Time is brief'). After taking in the jowl-dropping views and contemplating these wise words you'll probably want to crack on.

Trail of the Gods and other walks

The stunning coastline terrain is interspersed with old trails and mule tracks that provide many walking opportunities for most abilities. Early spring and early autumn may provide the mildest climatic conditions for trekking, but refreshments and suitable outdoor equipment are vital throughout the year. Many of the most popular routes are signposted but tricky trails on crumbly limestone paths make enlisting the expertise of a local walking guide such as **Giovanni Visetti** ① *Giovis, T339-694 2911, giovis.com*, a sensible choice. Giovanni leads trips along wild stretches of coastline near his home in Massa Lubrense as well as high up in the Monti Lattari, around Agerola and on the **Sentiero degli Dei** (Trail of the Gods). His website has lots of maps, descriptions and photos and is a portal for the region's outdoor specialists. Here he picks five of his favourite walks on the Sorrentine Peninsula and Amalfi Coast.

Giovanni's top walks

Termini to Punta Campanella to Termini This 7-km circular route can be enjoyed in both directions but Giovanni recommends the anticlockwise version which involves some scrambling on tricky limestone cliffs. From the main piazza in Termini follow the signs to Monte San Costanzo: walking on a tarmac road followed by a rough trail. On the way there are spectacular views of 16th-century watchtowers – Fossa di Papa and Torre Minerva at Punta Campanella – and beyond to the Bay of Ieranto and Capri. Between January and March there are vibrant blue swathes of *lithodora rosmarinifolia*, a native flower seen all along this coast.

Monte Faito and Molare This walk takes in an awe-inspiring limestone canyon with stratified rock layers and otherworldly rock formations. Take the cable car at Castellammare di Stabia to Monte Faito (1102 m) and then walk along a dusty trail through beech woods towards the Conocchia ridge, following the contours of the Vallone Acqua del Milo. An undulating path eventually climbs to the Molare, which at 1444 m is the highest peak in the Monti Lattari range.

Colli Fontanelle to Malacoccola to Torca There are numerous alternative routes along this awesome stretch of the Sorrentine Peninsula. One itinerary begins at the Colli Fontanelle and proceeds through chestnut woods and hillsides strewn with wild flowers to the promontory of Malacoccola, following the red and white signposts of the Alta Via dei Monti Lattari (Lattari Mountains High Route) to Torca. Fit walkers may like to complete a circular walk back to Colli Fontanelle through the Pineta delle Torre pine woods followed by a seat-of-the-pants descent down to the picturesque fjord of Crapolla.

Bomerano or Praiano to Colle Serra to Nocella (Trail of the Gods) According to Giovanni this is the classic *Sentiero degli Dei* (Trail of the Gods) and is best tackled westwards for the most awe-inspiring views of the Amalfi Coast. You can reach the pass of Colle Serra (580 m) from either Bomerano or Praiano, before taking in grassy terraces grazed by sheep and goats, fields studded with chestnut, oak and Mediterranean scrub, and then the limestone rock pinnacles and caves of the vast gorge Il Vallone di Grarelle. From the tiny village of Nocella (440 m) there is the option of rejoining the SS163 at Arienzo or more trekking adventures towards the towering cliffs of Montepertuso.

Valle dei Mulini aka Valle delle Ferriere (Valley of Mills) The full 6-km walk in the Valley of Mills passes through olive and lemon groves and fresh streams of the Canneto River. Picturesque stone mill buildings that once drove lime, water and paper production litter the often shady route. On the way you are likely to see local characters leading sack-laden donkeys. Fitter and adventurous walkers may relish the ridge walks of the higher trail from Pogerola to Scala.

Sorrentine Peninsula listings

For hotel and restaurant price codes and other relevant information, see pages 12-16.

🛏 Where to stay

All along the Sorrentine Peninsula and Amalfi Coast there is plenty of choice for most budgets, from lavish beachside hotels to out-of-the-way *agriturismi* up in the Lattari Mountains.

Self-catering

Among the companies offering affordable apartments and sumptuous villas are well-established brokers such as **Cuendet** (T0800-085 7732, cuendet.co.uk) and **CV Travel** (T0207-401 1010, cvtravel.co.uk). Smaller, local operations include **Amalfi Vacation** (T339-589 2551, amalfivacation. it) and **Amalfi Residence** (Largo Filippo Augustariccio 1d, 84011 Amalfi, Salerno, T089-873 588, amalfiresidence.it). **Coltur Suites** (T081-878 2966, coltursuites. com) have simply furnished apartments with terrace views over Sorrento's Marina Grande. Down at Marina del Cantone is the **Casale Villarena** (via Cantone 3, 80061 Nerano, T081-808 1779, casalevillarena.com) a largish complex containing a half-dozen apartments.

Sorrentine Peninsula *p24*

€€€€ La Minervetta, *Via Capo 25, Sorrento, T081-877 4455, laminervetta.com.* Full of colourful artworks and books, La Minervetta feels like a chic private home. Guest rooms have large windows with panoramic views, some have terraces with views.

€€€ Hotel Michelangelo, *Corso Italia 275, Sorrento, T081-878 4844, michelangelohotel. it.* The Michelangelo offers good value and modern yet attractive surroundings in busy and pricey Sorrento. Both public areas and the 121 guest rooms are bright with warm touches. There's a small pool and

a bar where barista Pepe supplies some entertaining quips.

€€ Grand Hotel Hermitage & Villa Romita, *Corso Sant'Agata 36, Sant'Agata sui Due Golfi, T081-878 0082, grandhotelhermitage.it.* It's not just the sublime views from the pool area and lush gardens that make these two adjoining and very differently styled hotels so special. The modern Grand Hotel offers great value, while the swankier Villa Romita, a former residence of a Neapolitan philosopher, has extra comfort and privacy.

€ La Ginestra, *Via Tessa 2, Santa Maria del Castello, Vico Equense, T081-802 3211, laginestra.org.* A bus passes nearby connecting with Vico Equense and Sorrento. Escape the tourist trails at this small farmstead-*agriturismo* up in the hills above Vico Equense. There are just seven rooms but all are cosy and of different sizes. Guests and daytime visitors can see the farm's goats, geese and deer. There's also a playground so it's great for families. The real bonus comes in the restaurant which serves La Ginestra's home-grown organic produce in classic Amalfitana dishes such as *scialatielli con pomodorini del Vesuvio* (pasta with tomatoes from the slopes of Vesuvius).

€ Seven H, *Via Iommella Grande 99, Sant'Agnello, T081-878 6758, sevenhostel. com.* A renovated *conservatorio* turned fancy hostel. A bed in a dorm costs around €27, while a comfy double is €100 in high season. The roof terraces have stylish loungers and sofas, and views.

Camping

Villaggio Nettuno, *Via A Vespucci 39, Nerano Massa Lubrense, T081-808 1051, villaggionettuno.it.* Isolation and beauty abound at enchanting Marina di Cantone, but there's no shortage of activities and seafood restaurants nearby. This dusty camping village has pitches for tents or caravans, as well as basic bungalows sleeping 2-8 people for €65-200 per night. Expect lots of activities (snorkelling, diving and boat trips), facilities (pool, sports and shop) and boisterous night-time shenanigans.

Sorrentine Peninsula *p24*

€€€€ Don Alfonso, *Corso Sant'Agata 11, Sant'Agata Sui Due Golfi, T081-878 0026, donalfonso.com. Tue-Sun 1200-1430, 2000-2300 (closed Wed in low season).* This place comes with two Michelin stars and a big reputation, but some Neapolitans reckon it's overrated and overpriced. Alfonso and Livia Iaccarino are celebrity food heroes in the south and organic produce pioneers: lots of their veg is grown on their Punta Campanella land while all the cheeses and fish come from local producers. Expect simply prepared dishes like fish casserole and caciotta cheese ravioli and an aubergine and chocolate creation, served in sumptuous rooms. Reservations recommended.

€€€€ L'Antica Trattoria, *Via Padre Giuliani 33, Sorrento, T081-807 1082.* Opened in 1930, this first-class restaurant with pergola-shaded terrace and elegant rooms is one for a special occasion. There's a great choice of menus, including tasting, veggie and gluten-free. Expect beautifully crafted seafood and meat dishes such as roast seabass and beef with aromatic crust.

€€ Antico Francischiello da Peppino, *Via Partenope 27, Massa Lubrense, T081-533 9780. Daily 1200-1530, 1830-2400, closed Wed in low season.* Set on a hillside between Sorrento and Massa, this popular restaurant filled with Sorrentine artworks serves the freshest seafood and grilled meats accompanied by the tastiest *contorni* (vegetables).

€€ Il Delfino, *Via Marina Grande 216, Sorrento, T081-878 2038. Daily 1200-1530, 1830-2230.* Down by the Marina Grande harbour this restaurant serves fresh seafood and pasta dishes including *fettuccine con gamberetti e spinaci* (pasta ribbons with spinach and prawns). Il Delfino's long modern *salone* is lined with picture windows giving sublime shoreline views while you dine.

€ Da Gigino Università della Pizza, *Via Nicotera 10, Vico Equense, T081-879 8426, pizzametro.it. Open 24 hrs.* The home of *pizza al metro* opened in the 1930s and claims to be the largest pizzeria in the world – it caters for as many as 2000 patrons at once. According to the experts a metre of pizza will feed five people but some of the Neapolitans regularly break the norm and some buttons. For the non-purists, antipasti and dolci are brought around on a trolley.

€ Pizzeria da Franco, *Corso Italia 265, Sorrento, T081-877 2066. Daily 1200-2400.* This no-nonsense pizzeria serves all the classics including margherita and *capricciosa* plonked on a tray in wax paper. Expect long queues.

Cafés and bars

Circolo dei Forestieri, *Via Luigi de Maio 35, Sorrento, T081-877 3263. Closed Feb-Mar.* This restaurant-bar has a large terrace with superb views, where you can hear traditional Neapolitan music live in the evening and more international tunes later on.

Gelateria Primavera, *Corso Italia 142, T081 807 3252.* Antonio Cafiero's famous parlour produces traditional and experimental ice cream flavours and outrageous cakes.

O Funzionista, *Via San Nicola 13, Sorrento.* Great for picnic snacks, refreshments, ice cream, chocolates and pastries.

Premiata Pasticceria Polli, *Corso Italia 172, Sorrento, T081-877 2889.* This pastry parlour is famed for its ice cream, *spremute di arancia* (fresh orange juice) and sweet treats including *bigne al caffè* (brioche with fruity fillings or Nutella) and *ciambelle* (doughnuts).

🎭 Entertainment

Sorrentine Peninsula *p24*
Clubs
Artis Domus, *Via san Nicola 56, Sorrento, T081-877 2073.* In the bricked-up bowels of a villa that once belonged to a Sorrentine scholar you can just about squeeze onto the dance floor where the smartly dressed locals lap up cheesy Italo dance and live music acts.

Music
Teatro Tasso, *Piazza Sant'Antonio, 25 Sorrento, T081-807 5525, teatrotasso.com.* Neapolitan folk music and dancing rocks the rafters of this renovated 1920s cinema building. The 75-minute Sorrento Musical Show does all the old *canzoni*, including *Funiculì funiculà*, *O' Sole Mio* and *Torna a Surriento*, and is accompanied by a meal.

Theatre
Cinema Teatro Armida, *Corso Italia 219, Sorrento, T081-878 1470, armida.eu.* Concerts, plays and cinema screenings are staged here. Matinee theatre productions of plays by Samuel Beckett or Eduardo de Filippo might be followed by the latest film release.

🛍 Shopping

Sorrentine Peninsula *p24*
Food and drink
Fattoria Terranova, *Piazza Tasso 16/18, T081-878 1263.* Outlet of the Sant'Agata sui due Golfi Agriturismo selling homemade jams, liqueurs, savoury conserves and oils.
Gelateria Latteria Gabriele, *Corso Umberto I 5, Vico Equense, T081-801 6234, gabrieleitalia.com.* As well as its famous gelati and *granite*, this place has all sorts of delicious goodies for picnics and to take home, including pastries, cheeses and olives.

Market
Mercato di Via San Cesareo, *Via San Cesareo, Sorrento.* Sorrento's weekly market, held each Tuesday, is good for picking up bargains like beach towels and beachwear.

Souvenirs
Gargiulo & Jannuzzi, *Via Fuori Mura 1, Sorrento, T081-878 1041.* G & J is world-renowned for marquetry goods (gorgeous boxes especially), elegant furniture and ceramics.

🏃 What to do

Sorrentine Peninsula *p24*
Boat trips
Coop Marina della Lobra, *T081-808 9380, marinalobra.com.* Boat trips from tiny Marina della Lobra to Sorrento, Capri, Positano, Amalfi and the marine reserve: Riserva Marina di Punta Campanella. For a few hundred euros you can hire a traditional *gozzo* sailing boat or one of their yachts for an afternoon.
Cooperativa San Antonio, *Via Cantone 47, Marina di Cantone, T081-808 1638.* This cooperative organizes boat trips around the nearby coves and as far as Capri.
Nautica O Masticiello, *Marina di Cantone, T081-8081443, masticiello.com.* Traditional *gozzo* sailing boats, motorized dinghies and flashy yachts can be hired here.

Cultural
City Sightseeing Sorrento, *Via degli Aranci 172, Sorrento, T081-877 4707, sorrento-city-sightseeing.it. Termini: piazza Lauro (Sorrento) and piazza Flavio Gioia (Amalfi).* This open-top sightseeing bus company now runs services along the coast, providing hop-on and jump-off tours along with multilingual commentary. They currently travel to and from Sorrento, Amalfi, Ravello, Maiori and Minori.

Diving

Diving Tour, *Via Fontanelle 18, Massa Lubrense, T081-808 9003, divingtour.it.* This well-established outfit organizes diving trips all over the world, including forays around their own beautiful backyard.

Diving Sorrento, *Via A Vespucci 39, Nerano, T081-808 1051, divingsorrento.com.* Based at the Nettuno Holiday Village at Nerano, Diving Sorrento offers PADI diving courses and snorkelling excursions. Check out the website for latest offers and details of basic accommodation available.

Tennis

Tennis courts can be booked at **Tennis Sorrento** (viale Montariello 4, Sorrento, T081-878 1246) and **Tennis Sport Sorrento** (via Califano, T081-807 4181). It's best to book early for cooler evening sessions in the summer.

Walking

Giovis, *Via 4 Novembre, Massa Lubrense, T339-694 2911, giovis.com.* Experienced hiking guide Giovanni Visetti leads guided walks on both coastlines and has a network of outdoor enthusiasts placed throughout the region. His website has plenty of information available, including maps, descriptions and photos. See page 28 for details of some of his favourite walks in the area.

⊖ Transport

Sorrentine Peninsula *p24*
Line 1 of the **Circumvesuviana railway** (T800-053939, vesuviana.it) stops along the Bay of Naples and Sorrentine Peninsula, terminating at Sorrento. From there seasonal hydrofoil services connecting all the resorts along both coasts are run by **Metro del Mare** (T199-600700, metrodelmare.net). **SITA** (T089-385 6494) runs buses to and from Naples, and there are many local lines reaching Ravello, Vietri and smaller hamlets. There are frequent Circumvesuviana trains to Napoli (1 hr), Pompei (30 mins), Ercolano (50 mins). Hydrofoil to Napoli (1 hr) and Capri (25 mins).

Bus and train stations are on Via Marziale, Sorrento, T800-053939/ T081-552 2176.

⊙ Directory

Sorrentine Peninsula *p24*
Money Banco di Napoli, Piazza Tasso 35, Sorrento, T081-807 3066 (ATM).
Medical services Ospedale, S Maria della Misericordia, Corso Italia, Sorrento, T081-533 1111. **Farmacia Alfani**, Corso Italia 129, Sorrento, T081-878 1226. **Post office** Corso Italia 210, Sorrento, T081-878 1495. **Tourist information** Sorrento office: piazza Tasso (via Luigi de Maio 35), Sorrento, T081-807 4033, sorrentotourism.com.

Amalfi Coast

The Amalfi Coast boasts the impossibly scenic coastal road, the SS163, otherwise known as the Amalfi Drive or *Via Smeraldo* (Emerald Road), which starts at Sant'Agata sui Due Golfi. This is connected to the SS145, *la Strada di Nastro Azzurro* (the Blue Ribbon Road), from Sorrento. Both roads glide around pulse-quickening bends offering visions of an azure and emerald sea down plunging limestone cliffs. Be warned: slow coaches and daredevil drivers of sports cars demand that you keep your eyes glued to the hairpins.

The SS163 soars above chic Positano's steep stairways and beaches before heading eastwards to Amalfi's maritime marvels and Byzantine Duomo. As an antidote to Amalfi's billowing tales of graft and glory on the high seas, you can climb 300 m to genteel and dreamy Ravello, whose refreshing air and garden vistas have inspired artists like Boccaccio and Wagner. The lush Dragone Valley is peppered with picturesque old mills. At Scala, Atrani, Minori, Cetara and Vietri majolica-tiled domes embellish the coast's natural wonders of fjord-like valleys, coves and limestone ridges as far as the city of Salerno.

Positano ➔ *For listings, see pages 41-45.*

Leaving the SS163, Viale Pasitea winds down into Positano, where traffic ceases and narrow lanes and *scalinatelle* (stairways) pass fragrant gardens and small boutiques. At via dei Mulini 23, Joachim Murat (1767-1815), Napoleon's brother-in-law and King of the Two Sicilies (1808-1815), built the imposing **Palazzo Murat** with its captivating *cortile* (courtyard). It's now one of the many swanky hotels here. Cool cotton threads and artisan-made sandals that hung on hipsters of the 1950s and 1960s still spill out of the shops on the way to Positano's jet-set playground, La Spiaggia Grande.

Chiesa di Santa Maria Assunta
ⓘ *Piazza Flavio Gioia, Positano, T089-875480. Daily 0800-1200, 1600-1900.*
The yellow, green, blue and white majolica Vietri tiles of the dome of Santa Maria Assunta dazzle near the beach and can be seen from all over Positano. The present triple-naved layout took shape in the 18th century when the church was built over the remains of a 13th-century Benedictine abbey. Inside, amid the underwhelming feast of white and gold stucco work, is *La Madonna Nera* (the Black Madonna), a Byzantine icon that holds centre stage during the town's exuberant *Festa della Assunta* (Feast of the Assumption), held each year on 15 August.

Spiaggia Grande and Positano's other beaches
Positano's main beach and ferry port, Spiaggia Grande, can be a seething mass of bodies and boat operators during the high season. Backed by restaurants and artists with easels, the western part of the shingle beach is public and free while bathing establishments cram the eastern half with parasols, loungers and deckchairs. Two defensive towers, Torre Trasita and Torre Sponda, frame this much-painted beach scene. A shady prom, via Positanesi d'America, runs along its cliffs and links with the the more secluded Spiaggia Fornillo which is less busy but has several beach bars.
    Serious sun-worshippers tend to walk to or hop on a boat to one of the small coves along the coast. These include La Porta (where Palaeolithic and Mesolithic remains were found in a cave), Fiumicello, Arienzo (film director Franco Zeffirelli had a villa here), San Pietro and Laurito (with restaurants and a hotel).

East of Positano ➔ *For listings, see pages 41-45.*

Praiano
Leaving Positano, to the west of Capo Sottile is the small village of Vettica Maggiore, whose main attraction is the peachy-looking **Chiesa di San Gennaro**, crowned with a majolica-tiled dome. Neighbouring Praiano, 6 km west of Positano, sits below Monte Sant'Angelo (120 m) and was the summer residence of the Amalfi Doge. Its watchtowers give it a mildly medieval atmosphere. As you approach, look out for the village houses set into the roadside rock – at Christmas these are lit up and turned into nativity scenes. Praiano's picturesque harbour and pebbly beach, Marina di Praia, lies within a small fissure between rocky cliffs. Nearby Gavitella beach has a tiny platform and an excellent seafood restaurant, La Gavitella Blu Bay (see page 42), accessed by tricky steps from Praiano or free shuttle boat from both Positano and Marina di Praia.

Furore

Continuing towards Amalfi on the SS163, it's worth stopping to admire the **Vallone di Furore**, a fjord-like gorge that cuts into the limestone rock below the Agerola plateau. The Furore gorge was known as Terra Furoris in ancient times after the almighty racket caused by the waves and wind whipping through the cleft in the towering rock walls. Gazing down at the dramatic ravine that gouges through the cliffs, you can see far below a couple of *monazzeni* (old fishermen's cottages) and a small pebbly beach filled with boats: the scene conjures up Peter Pan adventures and what JM Barrie called 'the nowhere village'.

The adventurous may enjoy approaching the fjord via the *Sentiero della Volpe Pescatrice* (Path of the Fishing Fox) from the old fishing village of **Furore**, which is now famed for its vibrant mural paintings. Other trails in the area have similarly evocative names (Mad-Bat Path, Crow's Nest Path, Path of Love). These paths offer various degrees of difficulty for walking, abundant local flora and fauna, and some intriguing buildings including three churches and old paper mills hugging the waters of a stream, the Schiato. The area makes an excellent base for walking in the Monti Lattari around Agerola and for sampling its local cheeses and Furore DOC wine. The Gran Furor Divina Costiera winery in Furore offers tours and tastings by appointment only (see page 44).

Agerola

On the Agerola plateau above Furore, amid the cows chomping on the lush meadows of the Monti Lattari, a more rural atmosphere reigns. Here you'll find spectacular walking trails (the Trail of the Gods passes through here) and new perspectives of Vesuvius. Some of Campania's finest cheeses, including *fior di latte* (cow's milk mozzarella) and *Provolone del Monaco* (well-aged cheese of stretched curd fashioned into ovoid balls) are produced on Agerola's fertile slopes.

Grotta dello Smeraldo

ⓘ *On SS163, 5 km west of Conca dei Marini. Mar-Oct 0900-1900, Nov-Feb 0900-1600, weather permitting, €6. Positano–Amalfi SITA buses stop nearby.*

This much-flogged boat trip amid natural blue-green waters and karst rock formations is too often spoiled by the kitsch additions. Arriving by road, the grotto is accessed by lift or a steep staircase, which may be dangerous for some; you can also get here by boat trip. The grotto measures 30 m x 60 m and is 24 m deep in places; a ceramic *presepe* (nativity scene) lies in its luminous depths.

Conca dei Marini

The dramatic defensive citadels, intimate marina and rocky cove of Conca dei Marini lie 5 km west of Amalfi. Conca's arresting combination of crystal clear waters backed by handsome palazzi perched on wild, towering cliffs make it a fabulous place to explore for a couple of hours. At the 14th-century **Monastero di Santa Rosa**, the nuns fashioned pastry into the shape of a priest's cowl and a special version of *sfogliatella* was born. Neighbouring Chiesa di Santa Maria di Grado contains lots of Baroque flourishes, Renaissance marble reliefs and a spooky sight: a reliquary containing the skull of San Barnaba.

Scala and Pontone

Perched on a lofty step near Ravello is the oldest settlement on the Amalfi Coast, the fortified village of Scala, whose origins go back to Roman times. At the end of the 13th century Amalfi's nobles built palaces including imposing Palazzo d'Afflitto and Palazzo Mansi, amid stone stairways that wind between citrus and chestnut groves. Scala's 12th-century **Duomo di San Lorenzo** ① *piazza Municipio 5, T089-857397, daily 0800-1300, 1800-1900*, has a Romanesque portal, majolica flooring and a crypt with wood carvings.

At the nearby village of Pontone is the **Centro Visite Valle delle Ferriere** ① *T089-873043, valledelleferriere.com*, where you can obtain maps and information about walking in the Valley of the Mills, which follows the force that drove the paper mills, the Canneto river (see page 29).

Amalfi and Atrani → *For listings, see pages 41-45.*

Back in the sixth century, Amalfi became a prosperous port, trading salt and slaves for eastern gold. This small Duchy of Naples rose rapidly, adding an archbishop and then maritime republic status in AD 987. Doges, laws, taxes and enormous wealth followed. Holy Roman Emperors, the Vatican and the rival republics were just a few of the behemoths to covet its commercial influence and affluence. In the 1340s a huge tsunami smashed the port and town, followed by a terrible plague, taking the wind out of Amalfi's sails.

Walking around this Unesco World Heritage site today, it's hard to believe that between the 9th and 12th centuries Amalfi's maritime empire rivalled Venice, Genoa and Pisa. It's well worth exploring the town's medieval lanes and exotic past, including the imposing Byzantine Duomo, although the buzz and bustle of its artisan paper shops and souvenir outlets may prove too taxing on a sweltering sunny day. Early mornings and late afternoons are the best times to appreciate Amalfi's commercial and artistic colours. Other favourite pastimes include swimming and sunbathing at one its pebbly beaches (choose from half-a-dozen private beaches belonging to hotels or the free public beach by piazza Flavio Gioia) and trips to savour lofty delights at Scala, Ravello and the Valle dei Mulini (Valley of the Mills).

Duomo
① *Piazza del Duomo, Amalfi, T089-871324. Summer 0900-2100, winter 1000-1700, €3 museum and cloisters, cathedral free.*
Dedicated to the apostle Sant'Andrea in the 9th century, Amalfi's cathedral reflects the maritime republic's oriental trading links in dazzling, Byzantine style. Its grand central staircase leads to a columned porch and bronze Byzantine doors above which towers a richly decorated façade (1203) and Romanesque campanile. The 13th-century Chiostro del Paradiso (Cloister of Paradise) has gardens surrounded by interlaced Arabic arches and a wavy roofline, while the museum contains 12th-century mosaics and an Angevin mitre studded with 19,000 pearls. Beside the nave is the frescoed Chapel of the Crucifix, the oldest part of the church, which leads to the crypt where part of Sant'Andrea's skull, looted from Constantinople during the Crusades, now resides.

Museo Civico
① *Town Hall, piazza Municipio, Amalfi, T089-873620. Mon-Fri 0830-1330, 1630-1830, free.*
Amalfi's civic museum contains the original manuscript that details the maritime code that governed the Mediterranean until 1570, *Il Tavoliere Amalfitane*. Exhibits relating to Flavio Gioia, the celebrated mariner and inventor of the dry compass, can also be seen. Down by the waterfront, in the piazza named after him, stands a statue of Flavio Gioia.

Museo della Carta

ⓘ *Palazzo Pagliara, via delle Cartiere 23, Amalfi, T089-830 4561, museodellacarta.it. Mar-Oct daily 1000-1830, Nov-Feb Tue-Sun 1000-1530, €5.*

Amalfi was one of the first places in Europe to bring back papermaking technology from the Orient and within this old paper mill the traditional methods are explained by a guide. The town remains one of the European capitals of *carta a mano* (hand-made paper) and the museum shop is full of posh stationery.

Atrani

A 20-minute walk east of Amalfi takes you away from the crowds to the more peaceful Atrani with its medieval buildings and atmospheric lanes interspersed with lush gardens. Amalfi's doges and judges lived here; the doges were crowned and buried at the 10th-century Chiesa San Salvatore de' Birecto (piazza Umberto 1): birecto being a reference to the doge's ceremonial cap. Down on the sheltered beach fishermen potter around with their *lampare* boats – these traditional vessels cast off at night covered in twinkling lights to attract fish.

Ravello → *For listings, see pages 41-45.*

Way up high at 350 m, some 6 km northeast of Amalfi, along a twisting, ear-popping road, is ever-so-refined Ravello. For nearly the entire second half of the last millennium Ravello's status as an independent principality meant that it was answerable only to the Pope. Prestigious villas and gorgeous religious buildings in Norman-Saracenic style sprang up amid elegant terraced gardens here in the 1400s. Illustrious visitors including Graham Greene, DH Lawrence, Wagner and JF Kennedy all found inspiration from its uplifting environs and views. Although the road to Ravello is often choked by traffic, all vehicles are left at the car park near piazza Duomo, where cafés, a ceramics shop and the elegant cathedral set the relaxed and detached-from-modernity tone. Allow at least three hours to enjoy Ravello's uniquely serene atmosphere.

Duomo

ⓘ *Piazza del Vescovado, Ravello, T089-858311. Cathedral daily 0900-1300, 1700-1900, museum Easter-Oct daily 0900-1300, 1500-1900. Cathedral free, €2 museum.*

The understated façade and elegant 13th-century campanile crowned with interlaced arches hint at the pleasing proportions of Ravello's cathedral. Inside, the intimate scale, exquisite artworks and refreshing lightness of it all make this a Romanesque duomo to remember. Built in 1086 and remodelled in 1786, the cathedral is dedicated to San Pantaleone – whose blood 'miraculously' liquefies without fail each 27 July. A double set of wooden doors protects enormous 12th-century bronze doors cast in Constantinople by Barisano da Trani. The panels on the doors depicting biblical scenes have been undergoing restoration. Medieval pulpits by Bartolomeo da Foggia have intricate bas-reliefs, vibrant mosaics and twisting columns resting on six squat marble lions. A mosaic of Jonah and the Whale recalls the frescoed panel by Giotto in Padova's Scrovegni Chapel. The series of frescoes of Madonna and Child here also appear to be influenced by Giotto's genius – Giotto did some work for the Angevins at Castel Nuovo in the 14th century. Descend into the crypt to see some pious relics, including a striking 13th-century marble bust of Sigilgaita Rufolo, wife of the treasurer of King Charles of Anjou (ruler of Naples 1265-1285) and depicted here as a Fortuna: a classical goddess symbolizing the city's prosperity.

Villa Rufolo

① *Piazza Duomo, Ravello, T089-857621. Daily 0900-1800, Apr-Sep until 2000, €5, €3 concessions.*

Built in 1270 by the Rufolos, a rich merchant family, this villa has hosted and inspired royalty, celebs and plebs. The 19th-century Scots botanist Francis Reid transformed a sadly neglected villa into the magical place we know today. If the dreamlike atmosphere created by Moorish arcades, cool cloisters and an ivy-covered tower don't grab you, the awe-inspiring views from the terraced gardens certainly will. Wagner's enchanting garden of Klingsor (from the opera *Parsifal*) was inspired by the villa and its surroundings, and it may even feature, in some way, in Boccaccio's *Decameron*. Classical music concerts and art shows are often staged here as part of the world famous Ravello Festival (see page 17).

Villa Cimbrone

① *Via Santa Chiara 26, Ravello, T089-857459. Gardens open daily 0900 to sunset, €6.*

A 10-minute walk along a hillside path from Piazza Duomo brings you to this fantastical castle that comes complete with turrets, cloisters, wonderful gardens and terraces with views to rival any in Italy. It was the brainchild of Ernest Beckett, 2nd Baron Grimthorpe, who in 1904 bought what was then little more than a ruined farmhouse and set about creating his masterpiece. The villa remained in the hands of the Beckett family until the 1960s, enchanting a succession of visitors that included Virginia Woolf, EM Forster, DH Lawrence, Henry Moore, Winston Churchill (who painted here), Greta Garbo and Gore Vidal. Although it's now a posh hotel, the gardens can still be visited during the daytime. Romantic verses by Roman poets and Persian astronomers are etched onto plaques among the fronds and flowers. Standing by the classical busts on the belvedere, there are exquisite views of the Gulf of Salerno and beyond.

Minori, Maiori and Tramonti → *For listings, see pages 41-45.*

Lying between Amalfi and Capo d'Orso, the two towns of Minori and Maiori can come as a bit of a disappointment after the glories of Ravello and Amalfi.

In **Minori** there's little evidence of its *cantieri*, the shipyards that helped to build the Amalfi maritime republic's fleet. Instead there's a small, scruffy beach backed by a promenade where market stalls manned by some dodgy characters sell cheap threads, odds and duds. Near the prom, the 11th-century **Basilica di Santa Trofimena** contains the relics of St Trofimena, in whose honour a festival is held each July.

Dusty remains of a Roman villa from the town of Regina Minor can be seen at Minori's **Villa Marittima** ① *via Capo di Piazza 28, T089-852893, Mon-Sat 0900 to 1 hr before sunset*, including some faded frescoes, a dank nymphaeum and some archaeological fragments. Terrapins sunbathe and perform bellyflops in the shallow courtyard pool here.

Minori's neighbour, **Maiori**, suffered a devastating flood in 1954 that washed away most of the town's charm, although it does have the majolica-tiled cupola of the 12th-century Chiesa di Santa Maria a Mare. Its large beach, strewn with flotsam and jetsam, is flanked by a long promenade.

Climb 600 m up the Valico di Chiunzi to the mountain villages around **Tramonti** for sublime views of seascapes and mountains. Mules carrying cheeses and fruits totter amid the tiny stone buildings. The people of Amalfi named the cold and dry wind that whipped them from the north, La Tramontana after its lofty neighbour.

Capo d'Orso

A few kilometres east of Maiori is Capo d'Orso, a protected reserve with jagged cliffs, a lighthouse and the **Abbazia di Santa Maria de Olearia** ① *open by appointment: contact Maiori tourist office T089-877452 for latest opening times*. This atmospheric monastery has chapels and caves hewn out of the limestone.

Erchie, Cetara and Vietri

Erchie has a small pebbly beach strewn with fishing boats while Cetara's beach is backed by a defensive tower and restaurants serving its famous *colatura di alici* (salted anchovy sauce similar to the ancient Roman garum) and tuna in oil. In the summer Vietri's Marina di Vietri is peppered with parasols and day-tripping Salernatini (Salerno is only 5 km away). The town's celebrated ceramics are everywhere: adorning cupolas and shopfronts, and spilling out of shops on via Madonna degli Angeli. An amazing 20,000 pots cover the eccentric, conical towers of iconic factory **Ceramiche Artistiche Solimne** ① *via Madonna degli Angeli 7, T089-212539*, designed by Paolo Soleri, a student of American modernist architect Frank Lloyd Wright. Nearby, in the village of Raito, is the **Museo della Ceramica** ① *Villa Giariglia, via Nuova Raito, T089-211835, museibiblioteche.provincia.salerno.it; Tue-Sat 0900-1315, 1400 to 1 hr before sunset in the summer €3*.

Amalfi Coast listings

For hotel and restaurant price codes and other relevant information, see pages 12-16.

● Where to stay

All along the Sorrentine Peninsula and Amalfi Coast there is plenty of choice for most budgets, from lavish beachside hotels to out-of-the-way *agriturismi* up in the Lattari Mountains.

Self-catering
Consider **Amalfi Vacation** (T339-589 2551, amalfivacation.it) and **Amalfi Residence** (Largo Filippo Augustariccio 1d, 84011 Amalfi, Salerno, T089-873 588, amalfiresidence.it). For affordable, bright apartments with terrace views try **Calante Luna** (Via Casa Cinque 4, Praiano,T339 7567960, calanteluna.it).

Amalfi Coast *p34*
€€€€ Hotel Santa Caterina, *Via Nazionale 9, 84011 Amalfi, T089-871012, hotelsantacaterina.it*. Clinging to the cliffs west of Amalfi this fabulous hotel is immersed in terraced gardens filled with citrus fruits and vines. A Bond-style lift whisks you down to the pool and shore where you can often watch the staff fishing for octopus. The best of the accommodation is in the annexe, where rooms have huge whirlpool baths and small terraces.

€€€€ Le Sirenuse, *Via C Colombo 30, Positano, T089-875066, sirenuse.it*. The Marchesi Sarsale opened up their noble residence in the 1950s, hosting the likes of John Steinbeck and many famous people since. Antiques and artworks fill the elegant public rooms, while the guest rooms have colourful tiled floors and vaulted ceilings – most have balconies with sea views. Talented Tuscan chef Matteo Temperini runs the stunning La Sponda restaurant.

€€€€ Palazzo Sasso, *Via San Giovanni del Toro 28, Ravello, T089-818181, palazzosasso. com*. Opened in 1997, this place regularly wins awards for its level of luxury and service. The breathtaking sea views from its lofty Ravello perch give this 12th-century palazzo the edge over many smart hotels on the *costiera*. Choose from the two-Michelin-starred Rossellini's restaurant or more laid-back Terrazza Belvedere. Facilities include a spa/wellness centre and heated pool and fitness area.

€€€ Marina Riviera, *Via P Comite 19, 84011 Amalfi, T089-871104, marinariviera. it*. Its vibrant tiles, great views and excellent staff make this a great base in Amalfi. The 20 guest rooms come in many shapes and sizes, most have sea views, and many have intimate balconies you can sit out on. Start the day eating breakfast on the terrace and perhaps spend a night at the amiable Gargano family's elegant Eolo restaurant nearby.

€€ Hotel Fico d'India, *Via Aldo Moro 2, Furore, T089-830520,hotelholidaysficodindia. com*. Exceptionally warm and welcoming family-run hotel with simply furnished rooms and sea views. Superb value and a handy Furore location for walkers.

€€ Hotel La Lucertola, *Via Cristoforo Colombo 29, 84019 Vietri sul Mare, T089-210255, hotellalucertola.it*. Recent refurbishment of this 1970s hotel on the Vietri coast has created a kind of value-for-money minimalist hotel: boutique on the cheap if you will. 33 guest rooms combine modern technology (Wi-Fi and Sky TV) with lots of 1980s-style black veneer, contemporary sinks and baths, plus sea views.

€€ Hotel Vittoria, *Via Fornillo 19, 84017 Positano, T089-875 049, hotelvittoriapositano. com*. Above the popular Spiaggia Fornillo is the Vittoria's flowery terrace, a great place to enjoy breakfast and their authentic *pizza* *napoletana*. Each of the 34 rooms has tiled floors, unfussy decor and a balcony with sea views. Expect tranquility and steep steps.

€ Il Castagno, *Via Radicosa 39, Fraz. San Lazzaro, Agerola, T081-802 5164, agriturismoilcastagno.com.* Immersed in the vineyards and chestnut trees of Agerola, this old farmhouse has simple but comfortable accommodation. Friendly owner Rosa Coccia organizes walking and cycling trips around the region.

🍴 Restaurants

Amalfi Coast *p34*

€€€ A Paranza, *Via Dragone, Atrani, T089-871840.* The name refers to a type of fishing net – expect fresh seafood served by knowledgeable, warm hosts. Famed for antipasti like stuffed courgette flowers and prawns with chickpea sauce. 10-minute walk from Amalfi along the road.

€€€ Da Gemma, *Via Fra Gerardo Sasso 9, Amalfi, T089-871345. Daily 1230-1445, 1930-2230.* Established in 1872, this well-respected ristorante still combines beautifully created dishes with a wonderful atmosphere. Try to book a table on the flower-filled terrace with views of the Duomo. Standout dishes include locally caught langoustines cooked in lemon oil and the classic *crostata Amalfitana* (baked tart). Reservations required.

€€€ Da Vincenzo, *Via Pasitea 172, Positano, T089-875128.* Friendly, family-run place popular with locals. Serves the day's catch – it could be octopus with potatoes, swordfish with peppers or fried calamari – alongside meat dishes and vegetarian *contorni*.

€€€ Hosteria Il Pino, *Via G Capriglione 13, Praiano, T089-874400.* Serene views over the Bay of Praiano combined with exquisite versions of seafood classics make for a memorable fine dining experience among the locals. Call for free shuttle serivvce.

€€€ La Gavitella Blu Bay, *Via Gavitella 1, Praiano, T089-813 1319, ristorantelagavitella. it. Daily 1200-1530, 1900-2230.* A small

boat whisks guests from Positano (Banchina di Approdo) and Marina di Praia to this elegant shoreline restaurant. Complementing the freshest seafood dishes is a wine list full of the region's best labels.

€€ Acquapazza, *Corso Garibaldi 33, Cetara, T089-261606. Daily 1230-1500, 1930-2300.* Cetara's famously fishy delights, including *colatura di alici* (anchovy sauce derived from an ancient Roman garum recipe), are served in this tiny place under a portico. Try *totani* (type of squid) with fennel seeds and *seppie* (cuttlefish) served with *fagioli* (beans) and the ubiquitous *colatura*. Reservations recommended.

€€ Da Lorenzo, *Via Fra Gerardo Sasso, Scala, T089-858290. Daily 1230-1500, 1900-2230 (closed Mon-Thu off season).* An attractive terrace with gorgeous views. Dishes include *paccheri con cuoccio* (large pasta tubes with gurnard) and *calamari fritti* (fried squid).

€€ Da Salvatore, *Via delle Repubbliche 2, Ravello, T089-857227. Apr-Oct daily 1230-1500, 1930-2300.* This is a good choice in the heart of Ravello. Book a table near the edge of the terrace and try their grilled *pescato del giorno* (catch of the day), with lots of freshly squeezed lemon juice. They also have some guest rooms.

€€ La Tagliata, *Via Tagliata 22, towards Montepertuso, Positano, T089-875872, latagliata.com. Daily 1230-1500, 1930-late.* Way up on the hill near Montepertuso this rustic trattoria run by Enzo, Peppino and friends is the most hospitable place to eat imaginable. They eschew seafood and plump for a menu full of local meats and vegetables. A good introduction to this simply prepared, tasty cuisine is their selection of antipasti but leave some room for their *semifreddi* (creamy cakes). Most afternoons the large picture windows are opened for the welcome breeze while evenings at La Tagliata involve cups of vino, music and carousing overflowing onto the wooden tables. Reservations are recommended.

€€ **Lido Azzurro**, *Lungo Mare dei Cavalieri,
Amalfi, T089-871384. Daily 1230-1500, 1930-
2230.* If you're after a no-frills trattoria, Lido
Azzurro serves outstanding-value pasta and
seafood dishes. Classic creations include
spaghetti alle vongole (with clams) and
tubetti con zucchini (tube-like pasta with
courgettes). Don't leave without trying the
local Furore DOC wine.

€€ **Lo Guarracino**, *Via Positanesi d'America
12, near Spiaggia Fornillo, Positano, T089-
875794. Daily 1200-1500, 1930-2330.*
Perched above the waves overlooking
Spiaggia Fornillo, this ristorante-pizzeria
serves great-value, thin-crust pizzas
baked in a wood-burning oven and
seafood dishes like *linguine guarracino*
(mixed seafood and little-tongued
pasta speciality). It's a hike along the
via Positanesi d'America path.

Cafés and bars

Andrea Panza, *Piazza Duomo 40, Amalfi,
T081-871065. Frutti canditi* (candied fruits)
fill the windows of this historic *pasticceria*
that dates back to 1830. Conveniently close
to the Duomo, it serves a refreshing *granite*,
gelati, cakes and pastries.

La Zagara, *Via dei Mulini 8/10, Positano,
T089-875964, lazagara.com.* All your
favourite Neapolitan pastries and
others including *crostatina fragolina*
(strawberry tart), plus savoury snacks,
cocktails and coffee, can be enjoyed to
the accompaniment of piano bar tunes
during the summer.

Sal De Riso, *Piazza Cantilena 1, Minori,
T089-853618, deriso.it.* A talented young
pastry chef Salvatore De Riso opened this
pasticceria up the road from his family's old
bar along the Minori seafront. His versions
of the classic pastries – such as *delizia
di limone* (lemon slice), *Babà al distillato
di rhum* and *profitteroles all'amaretto
disaronno* – are now renowned throughout
Italy. They also do artisan ice creams, *granite*
and a takeaway tray of devilish *dolci*.

Entertainment

Amalfi Coast *p34*
Clubs
Africana, *Via Terramare, Praiano,
T331-5330612, africanafamousclub.com,
2200-late.* You might spot a moustached-
Barney Rubble gyrating to cheesy dance
music on the glass-bottomed dance floor
here. Opened in 1962 this beach cave club
is like something out of a Connery-era
Bond movie.

Music on the Rocks, *Via Grotte dell'Incanto
51, Positano, T081-875874, musicontherocks.
it. Apr-Oct 2300-late, phone for latest listings.*
Soulful sounds and bangin' House are
the musical staples at this stylish club in
a vividly lit grotto. Expect fancy cocktails,
occasional celebrity sightings and steep
prices for drinks.

Music
Ravello Festival, *Viale Wagner 5, Ravello,
T089-858360, ravellofestival.com. Late Jun-
Oct.* A classical music and cultural festival
with lots of clifftop arias and Wagnerian
bombast. Highlight of the programme is
the *Concerto all'Alba* (dawn concert) on
10 August.

Suoni Degli Dei Associazione Pelagos,
*Via Casa Rispoli 4, Praiano, T089-874557,
isuonideglidei.com. Apr-Oct.* The more
laid-back alternative to the Ravello Festival
stages small classical concerts in gorgeous
natural settings along the famous *Sentiero
degli Dei* (Trail of the Gods).

Shopping

Amalfi Coast *p34*
Art and antiques
Amalfi nelle Stampe Antiche, *Piazza
Duomo 10, T089-873 6374, cartadiamalfi.
it.* Luigi d'Antuono's outlet is full of
hand-made Amalfi paper as well as lots of
interesting historic prints, books and maps.

Cartiera Amatruda, *Via delle Cartiere 100,
Amalfi, T089-871315, amatruda.it.* Amatruda

has been producing fancy paper products for generations and is a great place to get some special business cards made.

Ceramics
Ceramica Artistica Solimene, *Via Madonna degli Angeli 7, Vietri sul Mare, T089-210243, solimene.com*. The shop within this iconic factory has dinnerware to enliven the dreariest table scene. The rest of the street is crammed with colourful shops.
Ceramiche Autore, *Piazza Duomo 6, Ravello, T089-858260*. It's worth having a browse in this shop full of extravagantly coloured ceramics, next to the Duomo, if only to meet eccentric owner Pino.

Beachwear and clothing
La Botteguccia, *Via Trara Genoino 13, Positano, T089-811824*. Complete your Positano-style get-up with a pair of hand-made sandals from this outlet.
Sartoria Maria Lampo, *Viale Pasitea 12, Positano, T089-875021*. All the VIPs come to Maria's boutique filled with vibrant fabrics – it was the first shop to open after the Second World War and started the whole Positano fashionista scene.

Food and drink
Anastasio Nicola, *Via Lorenzo d'Amalfi, Amalfi, T089-871007*. Picnic supplies, snacks and refreshments near the Duomo.
I Sapori di Positano, *Via dei Mulini 6, Positano, T089-812055*. For all things citrus: limoncello, biscuits, candles, sweets and soap.

⚙ What to do

Amalfi Coast *p34*
Boat trips
Amalfi Boats, *Via Lungomare dei Cavalieri, Amalfi, T089-831890, amalfiboats.it*. Gioacchino and Flavio skipper the boat trips, ranging from tourist cruises to fishing forays. For the experienced there are various boats for hire.

Gennaro e Salvatore, *Via Trara Genoino 13, Positano, T089-811613, gennaroesalvatore. it*. Excursions to the Madonnina del Mare, Nerano and Li Galli.
Lucibello, *Via del Brigantino 9, Positano, T089-875032, lucibello.it*. Excursions around Capri, and along the coast to the Grotta dello Smeraldo, Amalfi and Praiano.

Cycling
Genius Loci, *Salerno, T089-791896, genius-loci.it*. This company organizes cycling and walking tours.

Food and wine
Gran Furor Divina Costiera Winery, *Via GB Lama 14, Furore, T089-830348, marisacuomo.com*. Tours and tastings by appointment. Andrea Ferraioli and Marisa Cuomo produce Costa d'Amalfi DOC wines using indigenous grape varieties including whites like Ripoli, Falanghina and Bianca Tenera, as well as hardy reds Piedirosso and Aglianco. Their gnarly vines grow on steep slopes studded with old stone walls, where even mules fear to teeter.
Mamma Agata and Ciao Laura Cookery Courses, *T1-615 426 1138/089-857845, ciaolaura.com/mammaagata.com*. American Laura Faust organizes various cookery courses on the Amalfi Coast, including Pizza Pie in the Sky at Ravello with Mamma Agata (€175), who has cooked for Sinatra and the Kennedys.

Walking
Maurizio De Rosa, *84010 Praiano, T339-171 8194, sulsentierodeglidei.it*. Walking tours around Valle delle Ferriere, Monte Faito, Punta Campanella and Sentiero degli Dei. Maurizio tailors his excursions to suit most abilities and needs, and even has an interesting alternative to the classic Trail of the Gods which starts at Vettica Maggiore and visits the San Domenico monastery at 400m.

⊖ Transport

Amalfi Coast *p34*
Prepare yourself for traffic on the roads along the Amalfi Coast, especially on the SS163, which is very narrow in places and often gets jammed with coaches from May to October.

In the summer, the most comfortable way to reach Positano, Amalfi and Minori is to take a hydrofoil from Napoli Molo Beverello. There are also seasonal services connecting resorts along the both the Sorrentine and Amalfi coasts run by **Metro del Mare** (T199-600700, metrodelmare. com). **SITA** (T081-552 2176) runs buses to and from Naples, and there are many local lines reaching Ravello, Vietri and smaller hamlets. There's a bus station on Piazza Flavio Gioia, Amalfi, T089-871016.

⊕ Directory

Amalfi Coast *p34*
Money Banco di Napoli, piazza Duomo 1, Amalfi, T089-871005, ATM. **Medical services Croce Rossa Italiana**, via Nuova Chiunzi 1, Maiori, T089-852002. **Farmicia del Cervo**, piazza Duomo 42, Amalfi, T089-871045. **Post office** Corso delle Repubbliche Marinare 33, Amalfi, T089-830 4811. **Tourist information AAST**, via delle Repubbliche Marinare, Amalfi, T089-871107, amalfitouristoffice.it.

Salerno and Paestum

Campania's second city, Salerno, located 55 km southeast of Naples, is a busy university town with some fine historic sights and a scenic *lungomare* (seaside promenade). Since its foundation in the sixth century BC, Salerno has had as many rulers as Naples. In recent times, it was the focus of frenzied skirmishes from 1943 to 1945 between the Allies, Germans and retreating Fascists. Amid the post-Second World War modernist architecture are remnants of a medieval quarter, 19th-century buildings and art nouveau palazzi. Some 40 km south of Salerno on the flat plains of the Sele River are the impressive Graeco-Roman ruins of Paestum. An archaeological museum here tells the fascinating story of a lost civilization, while 9 km up the road, amid grazing buffalo, are more Greek temple remains at the *Santuario di Hera Argiva*.

There are fabulous sea views along the recently revamped, palm tree-lined *lungomare*. At its western end is the Villa Comunale, with its verdant gardens flanked by historic buildings. The *centro storico* starts near the flamboyant Teatro Verdi building (see page 51). Beyond the smart shops on via di Porta Catena is the piazza Sedile del Campo, the old market square, which contains the spouting dolphins of La Fontana dei Delfini and arcaded palaces including Baroque Palazzo dei Genovesi (a university seat and cultural venue). Nearby via dei Mercanti turns into corso Vittorio Emanuele, Salerno's main shopping street.

Duomo di San Matteo
ⓘ *Piazza Alfano 1, Salerno, T089-231382. Daily 1000-1800, free.*
Salerno's cathedral was founded in AD 845, rebuilt in 1076, and has been renovated many times since. A Romanesque gateway leads to a Moorish atrium containing 28 columns pinched from Paestum. Towering 55 m above the beautiful colonnade is the cathedral's striking 12th-century campanile. A bronze door with niello engraving from Constantinople (1099) leads into the elegant Latin-cross interior with its two *ambones* (medieval raised platforms/pulpits). Down in the crypt is the body of the evangelist St Matthew and among the Roman and medieval sarcophagi is the tomb of Pope Gregory VII who died in exile in 1085. The adjoining Museo Diocesano contains an exquisite 11th-century altar-front with ivory panels.

Chiesa di San Benedetto
ⓘ *Via San Benedetto 38, Salerno, T089-231135. Mon-Sat 0900-2000, free.*
Grand interiors of the 11th-century wing of the San Benedetto convent are overflowing with antiquities organized into themed sections. There are fascinating finds from Roman Salerno (seek out the 1st century bronze head of Apollo found in the gulf in 1930) and some fifth-century burial treasures from Roscigno.

Castello di Arechi
ⓘ *Via Benedetto Croce, Salerno, T089-233900, castellodiarechi.it. Mon-Fri 0830-1930, Sat-Sun 0900-1330, free.*
Take a taxi or climb the steep path to this castle for fabulous views of the Gulf of Salerno. The impressive fortifications were built by Byzantines and added to by the Normans, Angevins and Aragonese. A museum contains collections of weapons, ceramics, armoury, glass and coins. Occasional concerts and firework displays light up the battlements.

Paestum is about 40 km south of Salerno. By car, take the A3 autostrada and exit at Battipaglia (from the north) or Eboli (from the south) and follow the signs. The train from Salerno takes 35 minutes and the SCAT bus from piazza della Concordia in Salerno takes 80 minutes. The entrance is a 10-minute walk from the station. During the summer months the Metro del Mare from Naples or Amalfi stops at nearby Agropoli, from where a bus serves Paestum.

Mainland Italy's most important Greek ruins and its three impressive Doric temples emerge out of the grassy Sele River plain, a place famed for its wild roses and violets back in antiquity. Poseidonia was founded by Greek settlers from Sybaris around 600 BC and continued to thrive under Lucanian tribes (from 410 BC) and then the Romans (273 BC), who renamed it Paestum. Poets Ovid and Virgil sung Paestum's praises before Saracen invasions and encroaching malarial swamps drove its inhabitants into the mountains. Its architectural splendours were spared looting as it became enveloped in overgrown mire and was largely forgotten about, only to be rediscovered in the 18th century when engineers excavated a road straight through the amphitheatre. Thereafter, Grand Tourists and arty adventurers like Shelley, Canova and Goethe made it the climax of their European odysseys. It was not until the 1950s that major archaeological digs started to unearth the minutiae of ancient treasures. Allow a full day if you want to get the most out of a visit to this wonderfully evocative site.

Gli Scavi di Paestum
ⓘ *Archaeological area open daily 0900 to 1 hr before sunset, €4 or €6.50 combined ticket with museum.*
Entering through the porta della Giustizia, one heads north along the **Via Sacra** (Sacred Road) that linked the principal buildings of Poseidonia with the **Tempio di Hera** (Temple of Hera), Paestum's oldest structure, built in 550 BC. Its 50 tapering outer columns were given convex curves to give the illusion of straight lines from a distance, a process known as *entasis*. The survival of these bulging columns makes this the most well-preserved example of an early Doric temple anywhere. Seek out the sacrificial altar and a square well where the sacrificial remains were thrown.

Next to the Temple of Hera is Paestum's largest temple, the **Tempio di Nettuno** (Temple of Neptune), built around 450 BC. Its covering of Travertine marble makes the temple glow a rich hue at sunset. Confusingly, historians believe that it was dedicated to Hera Argiva, goddess of fertility. It is 6 m longer than the Temple of Hera, with 36 fluted columns (six at each end and 14 along the sides). Look carefully at the cornices and horizontal lines that curve slightly upwards in the middle: this architectural method creates an elegant appearance and less sagging look. To the east are the remains of a sacrificial altar.

Continuing along the via Sacra, the Roman Forum is one of the most complete anywhere in the world. A Doric portico surrounded it. To the north is the 1st century BC amphitheatre, which is cut in half by a modern road. The rectangular buildings next to the forum had various uses: *taberna* (shops), a *comitium* (court), basilica, *macellum* (covered market) and temples dedicated to Asclepius (the god of healing) and Fortuna Virilis (where women worshipped Venus).

The **Tempio di Cerere** (Temple of Ceres), further north, is really an Athenaion: a temple dedicated to the goddess Athena. Three Christians tombs were added in the medieval period. It has 34 fluted columns and is the smallest of the three temples.

To the west of via Sacra there was a large residential district containing some luxurious homes, some with pools. A tour of the city walls throws up more intriguing finds and layers of history including towers, bastions and medieval watchtowers.

Museo Archeologico Nazionale
ⓘ *Via Magna Grecia 917, Paestum, T0828-811023, infopaestum.it. Daily 0830-1845 (closed on first and third Mon of each month), €4 or €6.50 combined ticket, reductions with Artecard.*
Paestum Archaeological Museum, designed in 1952, is just over the road from the

excavations, near the tourist office. Top billing goes to the Tomb of the Diver, comprising frescoed panels including a funereal banqueting scene and the famous image of a youth diving gracefully into blue water, an allegory of death. Among the burial treasures, architectural fragments and terracottas from Paestum's Greek, Lucanian and Roman eras is sculpture depicting various Homeric scenes found at the sanctuary of Hera Argiva.

Museo Narrante del Santuario di Hera Argiva
ⓘ *Masseria Procuriali, T0828-861440, infopaestum.it. Daily Tue-Sat 0900-1600, free.*
At the mouth of the Sele river, 9 km north of Paestum, is the Sanctuary of Hera and a new, engaging multimedia museum that spills the ancient beans and beads about ancient Greek cults and their penchant for weaving and spinning. Ancient scribes Strabo (63 BC – AD 26) and Pliny the Elder (23 BC – AD 79) wrote about this legendary place which according to Magna Grecia mythology was built by Jason and the Argonauts. Earthquakes, eruptions and conflicts smashed the lavish temples, then the increasingly marshy Sele plain and looting left us mere foundations to stumble upon. In 1934 it was discovered by archaeologists and although little remains of its former grandeur it's an evocative place to visit and a big, wallowing hit with grazing buffalo.

Tenuta Vannulo
ⓘ *Via G Galilei (Contrada Vannulo), Capaccio Scalo, T0828-724765, vannulo.it.*
You can get up close to the mud-wallowing buffalo on a guided tour of the estate and dairy on this farm near Paestum. As well as producing arguably the best mozzarella in the world, the creative Palmieri family also sell ricotta, served here with a choice of condiments (cinnamon, honey, cocoa powder, nutmeg and kumquat jelly), and yoghurts (flavoured with local figs, hazelnuts and pomegranate). They also make delicious organic buffalo-milk ice cream and handbags made from buffalo hide.

Salerno and Paestum listings

For hotel and restaurant price codes and other relevant information, see pages 12-16.

🛌 Where to stay

Salerno and Paestum *p46*

€€€ Il Cannito, *Via Cannito, Capaccio, Paestum, T0828-196 2277, ilcannito. com.* Traditional stone dwellings near Paestum's archaeological site have been converted into a relaxing rural retreat full of stylish design flourishes. Whitewashed guest rooms have all the technology and comforts including air-conditioning, underfloor heating and LCD TVs, and minimalist bathrooms have hydro-massage baths. A free shuttle bus takes guests to a nearby beach and there are lots of walks to be had in the surrounding woods.

€€ Oleandri Resort Hotel Residence Villaggio Club, *Via Laura 240, Paestum, T0828-851730, residenceoleandri.com.* Pools with swaying palms, extensive lush gardens leading to the beach and sports facilities makes this resort especially suited to families. There are 53 rooms and lots of accommodation options including suites and villas for up to seven people. Food can be eaten at the poolside restaurant or else you can buy provisions and cook in your kitchenette. Sports and activities such as beach volleyball, ping-pong or whiff-whaff, and aerobics workouts are organized daily. It's isolated so you need a vehicle.

€€ Olimpico, *Pontecagnano-Salerno, T089 203 004, hotelolimpico.it.* A well-kept resort hotel between Salerno and Paestum. Expect unfussy modern rooms, restaurant, beach, pool and facilities aplenty. A good option for those driving (it's out of the way).

🍴 Restaurants

Salerno and Paestum *p46*

€€€ Cenacolo, *Piazza Alfano I 4, Salerno, T089-296 5482. Tue-Sun 1230-1500, Tue-Sat*

1930-late. Il Cenacolo is a well-respected ristorante Salernitano, with elegant rooms over the road from the Duomo. The cuisine is based on traditional regional dishes given an innovative twist. Start with the *crespelle* (folded and filled savoury crêpes) and perhaps try one of their rustic creations, like the vegetable pie or the classic *parmigiana di melanzane* (layered aubergine, cheeses and tomatoes) which here is given a salty, tangy edge with anchovy. Reservations recommended.

€€ Antica Pizzeria del Vicolo della Neve, *Vicolo della Neve 24, Salerno, T089-225705. Thu-Tue 1930-late.* Salerno's oldest pizzeria (going strong for over 150 years) is based next to a 10th-century church. Its old vaulted cellars were once crammed with compacted snow and preserved fish – the traditional food served here mirrors these atmospheric surroundings. Expect classic pizzas and *calzone*, as well as *polpette* (meat balls), *baccalà e patate* (salted cod and potatoes) and *carciofi e peperoni ripieni* (filled artichokes and peppers with meaty fillings).

€€ Nettuno, *Zona Archeologica, via Nettuno, Paestum, T0828-811 028. Apr-Sep daily 1200-1500, Oct-Mar Tue-Sun 1200-1500.* These rustic yet refined 19th-century dining rooms fill with passing tourists and locals who lap up the excellent value *crespolini* (large savoury crêpes) filled with local mozzarella, and the magical views of the ancient temples. It's run by the Pisani family who opened the doors of this famously isolated villa as a restaurant in 1929 and continue to create seafood favourites like *ricciola* (amberjack fish) served with the pepperminty herb *calamintha* and some mighty fine home-made desserts.

Cafés and bars

Pantaleone, *Via Mercanti 75-77, Salerno, T089-227825.* Opened in 1868, Salerno's famous *pasticceria-gelateria* is renowned for its trademark *scazzetta* (*pan di spagna* sponge, sweet *crema*, strawberries and topped with a candied strawberry) as well as a creamy *delizia al limone* and all the Parthenopaean pastry classics like *babà* and *sfogliatella*.

⊙ Entertainment

Salerno *p47*
Teatro Verdi, *Piazza Luciani, Salerno, T089- 662141, teatroverdisalerno.it.* Salerno's lavishly decorated theatre, built in the 1860s, has exquisite medallions honouring artistic greats including Dante Alighieri, Giotto and Da Vinci. Tickets for concerts and other performances start at €12.

⊙ Shopping

Salerno *p47*
Casa Bianca, *Corso Garibaldi 231, Salerno, T089-232125.* Lots of Campanian cheeses and salami to fill your panini, as well as some cooked foods for a special picnic on the Salerno *lungomare*.

⊖ Transport

Salerno *p47*
Ferry and hydrofoil services from Naples, Capri, Ischia and all along the coast. Train from Naples (1 hr) and from Paestum (35 mins).

Contents

54 Capri
55 Capri Town
56 *Map: Capri*
57 Anacapri and around
60 Listings

64 Ischia
65 Ischia Porto and
Ischia Ponte
67 *Map: Ischia*
66 Around the island
68 Listings

72 Procida
73 Marina Grande and
Terra Murata
74 *Map: Procida*
75 Listings

Footprint features

57 Bathing spots on Capri
59 Walks on Capri

Capri, Ischia & Procida

Capri

Capri is just 5 km from Punta della Campanella on the Sorrentine Peninsula. Despite the invasion of day-trippers who throng its boutique-lined lanes and cram its cute orange buses, Capri still has that special allure, particularly in its gorgeous hidden bays beloved of emperors and film stars and along its tranquil, flower-strewn paths. Out of season and after the last boat to Naples has departed you almost feel part of the privileged Capri set. Its chic epicentre is Capri Town, 142 m above sea level and 3 km by road from the island's main harbour, Marina Grande, which is always abuzz with the weaving and heaving of foaming boats, floppy-hatted tourists and *facchini* (porters). Anacapri, 3 km to the west by road, is less self-consciously exclusive and has a friendlier feel. The single-seat chairlift ride to Monte Solaro is a magical, must-do experience – from its summit there are wonderful walks across wild country.

Capri Town sits in a lush bowl between the limestone cliffs of Monte Solaro and Punta del Capo. Known as **La Piazzetta** (the little square), piazza Umberto I is the intimate and chic social hub of Capri Town and the island. Everyone, anyone and no one over the past two centuries has sat at one of the cafés here, plonking their feet on the flagstones and glancing intermittently over a newspaper to do some people-watching – you never know who will walk by. It must have been a less pricey pleasure, though, for the likes of Dickens, Greene, Gorky and Lenin.

Gaze beyond the entertaining ebb and flow and you'll see the **Torre dell'Orologio** (clock tower), with its majolica-tiled clock face; the **Municipio** (town hall); the Baroque **Chiesa di Santo Stefano** (with fragments of Roman flooring from Emperor Tiberius's Villa Jovis); and **Palazzo Cerio** ① *T081-837 6218, Tue-Wed, Fri-Sat 1000-1300, Thu 1500-1900*, which has natural history collections amassed by naturalist and physician Ignazio Cerio.

A maze of medieval *vicoli* (alleyways) fans out from the Piazzetta. Via Madre Serafina, an atmospheric arcaded street, follows the town's old ramparts. Between the whitewashed buildings light-wells offer glimpses of flowery terraces. The locals would pour hot oil through the holes onto invading Saracen pirates. Via Lungano and Capri's main via Vittorio Emanuele III are lined with boutiques, bars, *pasticcerie* and glitzy hotels, including Il Quisisana (meaning 'here one heals'), originally a 19th-century sanatorium founded by a Scottish doctor.

Certosa di San Giacomo

① *Via Certosa, T081-837 6218. Tue-Sun 0900-1400, free.*
The Charterhouse, a 14th-century Carthusian monastery dedicated to the apostle Giacomo (James), is located southeast of the Piazzetta. The monks have long since packed their habits, but the serene atmosphere, sombre architecture and verdant gardens makes it worth the walk here. It's rather run down but there are things to see: two cloisters, a church, panoramic terraces and the intriguing refectory museum that contains Roman statues recovered from the Grotta Azzurra and haunting paintings by the German painter, Wilhelm Diefenbach.

Continuing on via Giacomo Matteotti you come to the **Giardini di Augusto** (Gardens of Augustus), a vibrant profusion of flowers and vegetation with jowl-dropping terrace views to die for – so mind the chasm.

Belvedere Cannone

From the Piazzetta, follow the via Madre Serafina, linger at the Santa Teresa church, then climb to the impressive Castiglione (a sprawling €40 million villa still up for sale at time of writing). Steps lead to the belvedere that looks over the Faraglioni rocks, the Charterhouse, the Grotta delle Felci (where Bronze Age artefacts were found) and down towards the Marina Piccola.

Circular coastal walk from the Piazzetta

Starting at the Piazzetta, take via le Botteghe, then follow via Croce and via Matermania –before following the signs to steps that descend near the breathtaking natural archway, **Arco Naturale**. A path continues to the **Grotta di Matermania** – a cave with a Roman *nymphaeum* and lots of *opus reticulum* bricks. At the craggy outcrop **Punta Masullo** you'll

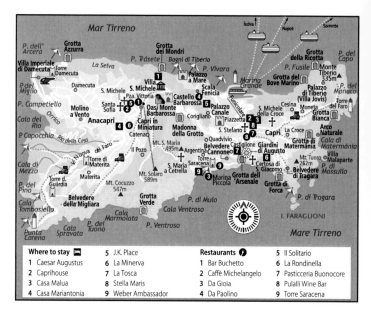

Where to stay 🛏		Restaurants 🍴	
	5 J.K. Place		5 Il Solitario
1 Caesar Augustus	6 La Minerva	1 Bar Buchetto	6 La Rondinella
2 Caprihouse	7 La Tosca	2 Caffè Michelangelo	7 Pasticceria Buonocore
3 Casa Malua	8 Stella Maris	3 Da Gioia	8 Pulalli Wine Bar
4 Casa Mariantonia	9 Weber Ambassador	4 Da Paolino	9 Torre Saracena

glimpse red-hued **Villa Malaparte** with its trapezoidal staircase and angular shapes: this piece of Italian rationalist architecture was named after its eccentric owner, the writer Curzio Malaparte. It starred alongside Brigitte Bardot in Jean-Luc Godard's 1963 film *Le Mépris*. Climbing up to **Punta Tragara**, there are fabulous views of the Faraglioni and Monacone rocks rising from turquoise waters. Head northwest along leafy via Tragara to return to the Piazzetta. Allow at least three hours to do the entire route.

Villa Jovis and Il Salto di Tiberio
ⓘ *Viale Amedeo Matiuri. Daily 0900 till dusk.*

Villa Jovis, Emperor Tiberius's infamous 7000-sq-m palace from which he ruled the Roman Empire from AD 27 to 37, takes about an hour on foot to reach from Capri Town. Verdant lanes pass by colonnaded gardens (linger at Villa La Moneta at via Tiberio 32), prickly pears, abundant birdlife and lounging lizards. There's not much left of the lavish apartments (although Prime Minister Silvio Berlusconi had plans to allow luxury pads to be built here for him and his mates). Between orgies, gorging and torturing, Tiberius apparently enjoyed spending time in the loggia, with its sublime views, and in the *specularium*, where astrologers gave him the low-down perhaps. Within the site, at Monte Tiberio, there's a rustic church, **Santa Maria del Soccorso**, scene of the Festa di Santa Maria del Soccorso (7-8 September), a festival involving morning mass, music and dance.

Tiberius's Leap, near Villa Jovis, is a 300-m cliff from where the emperor apparently flung his tortured victims. According to the Roman historian Gaius Suetonius Tranquillus, sailors would wait in the sea below to finish off the unfortunates. Suetonius flung a lot of juicy muck in his opus *The Lives of the Twelve Caesars*, and a reputation for perversion, madness and cruelty has certainly stuck to Tiberius.

Bathing spots on Capri

Marina Piccola Capri's most famous bathing spot, on the south side of the island, is split into two small bays, the **Marina di Pennauro** and **Marina di Mulo**, which overlook the Scoglio delle Sirene (Sirens' Rock) and Faraglioni Rocks. Shoreline seafood restaurants with wooden decks, including Da Gioia (see page 61), look over tiny pebbly beaches and bathing establishments that fill from 0800 in the summer.

Bagni di Tiberio West of Marina Grande is this intimate cove with the remains of one of Tiberius's villas and a Roman theatre. Take the shuttle boat from Marina Grande or a winding path that starts five minutes' walk above the JK Place Hotel. There are beach huts, a small pebbly beach and a seafood restaurant/bar Bagni di Tiberio, run by Carlo di Mattino, who can be seen here mending his nets off season. From August, the cliffs of Anacapri block out much of the sun so sun-worshippers prefer it in early summer.

Bagni Nettuno Backed by dramatic cliffs, this picturesque rocky shoreline near Anacapri has a popular bathing establishment (via Grotta Azzurra, T081-837 1362) with two pools (for adults and kids) and a bar-ristorante, and rents out deckchairs, parasols and cabins from late March to mid-November. A bus service shuttles bathers to and from Anacapri.

Lido di Faro A winding road from Anacapri reaches the southwest extremities of the island and Lido di Faro or Punta Carena (T081-837 1798, lidofaro.com). Amid the sun-worshippers and boulders, there's a snack bar (Da Antonio's) and sun terrace built onto the jagged rocks near the lighthouse. Migliara cliffs soar 292 m above the snorkellers, divers and dive-bombers who enjoy the deep pools and marine life here – be careful of the sharp limestone rocks.

Spiaggia di Marina Grande Capri's largest beach is handily placed, just a short stroll west of the port-side bustle. Around 100 m of popular pebbly beach stretches to cliffs and breakwater rocks below the swanky J.K. Place hotel. There are a couple of establishments with facilities, snack bars and public access, so it's ideal for day-trippers seeking a dip and doze *alla caprese* before catching the return boat.

Anacapri and around

Sitting below Capri's highest point, Monte Solaro, Anacapri – a short bus ride from Capri – has a friendlier, more villagey feel than self-consciously chic Capri Town.

Piazza della Vittoria is always abuzz with buses, taxis, coaches and crowds. Up its steps is the chairlift to Monte Solaro, Villa San Michele and viale Axel Munthe lined with perfumed boutiques and aristocratic *alberghi*. Anacapri's main lane via Orlandi heads past some interesting shops and friendly *chiaccheroni Anacapresi* (local chit-chatters) to an intimate piazza in front of the cheery, yellow-hued **Chiesa di Santa Sofia**, a favourite meeting place and wedding venue. On the way is the **church of San Michele** (with majolica marvels) and **Casa Rossa**, a building painted in Pompeian red with Moorish detailing, a gallery of Caprese landscape paintings and a courtyard displaying archaeological fragments. Along the craggy northwestern and western coastline are some magical natural and ancient attractions including the ethereal Grotta Azzurra cave and the fort, flora and fauna-studded trail, *Il Sentiero dei Fortini*.

Chiesa San Michele
ⓘ *Piazza San Nicola, Anacapri. Daily 0930-1800, €1.*
Built in 1761, the Baroque church has majolica flooring depicting Adam and Eve in a dreamlike scene, viewed from a special gallery. The beguiling small square here is a meeting place for the Anacapresi.

Villa San Michele
ⓘ *Viale Axel Munthe 34, Anacapri, T081-837 1401, villasanmichele.eu. Mar 0900-1630, Apr and Oct 0900-1700, May-Sep 0900-1800, Nov-Feb 0900-1530, €6.*
Swedish doctor and writer Axel Munthe (1857-1949) created this idyllic villa with an emphasis on bringing out the island's "light, light everywhere". After assisting the cholera epidemic relief effort in the 1880s, he put down his stethoscope and focused on constructing the villa's buildings and lush garden, with its loggia, pergolas, statues and columns, and a circular viewpoint with the most stunning views across the Gulf of Naples. Run as a museum by the Axel Munthe Foundation, temple-like interiors display Munthe's eclectic collection of art, antiquities, bric-a-brac and personal memorabilia. There are also the remains of a Roman imperial villa. Munthe's *The Story of San Michele*, published in 1929, charts his Caprese love affair and became a worldwide bestseller, drawing many a pilgrim to this enchanting place.

Monte Solaro chairlift
ⓘ *Seggiovia Monte Solaro, via Caposcuro 10, T081-837 1428. Mar-Oct 0930-1730, Nov-Feb 1030-1500, €10 return, €7.50 single, free for children up to 8 years.*
If you don't fancy the walk, the chairlift offers a quick and easy means of reaching the highest point of the island. Feet dangle over a hiking path weaving through terraced gardens dotted with quirky ornaments and abundant produce, and as you rise to the 600-m summit the craggy ridge, wild parched landscape and shimmering seascapes become ever more spectacular. After 12 minutes you arrive just below the one-bar terrace which is pleasingly slightly run-down. You can spend a couple of hours sitting in a deckchair slurping ice cream and exploring the rough terrain and knee-knocking drops, including the vertiginous cliffs down to Ventroso and limpid blue waters. Just watch your step though. There are lots of walks from here: to Monte Capello, the small church at Cetrella and along the very tricky Passetiello path back to Capri Town (note that the Passetiello has lots of loose rocks and steep scrambles, so should only be tackled with an experienced guide).

Grotta Azzurra
ⓘ *0900 till dusk. Bus or by foot (3 km) from Anacapri, or boat from Marina Grande, then entry to the cave by rowing boat.*
Once filled with statues from Tiberius's Gradola villa, the Blue Grotto and its ethereal light atmospherics were 'rediscovered' in 1826 and turned into a Grand Tour day trip. The lighting effects inside the cave are caused by the refraction of the sun's rays in the waters, lighting the cave from below in an eerie shade of blue. The island's most popular tourist attraction can be approached via a footpath, lift or by boat, with many excursions around

Walks on Capri

Below, walking guide Giovanni Visetti has picked his favourite Caprese walks, the first three of which are best tackled going uphill as they contain tricky and steep sections with loose rocks. None of these trails should be attempted in bad weather. For more information, maps and contact details of Capri guides check out giovis.com and whenever.it.

Anacapri to Monte Solaro This spectacular trail starts at the circular defensive tower Torre della Guardia, rebuilt by the English during the conflicts with Murat's republican French troops 200 years ago, passing the Belvedere di Migliera and verdant slopes of Monte Cocuzzo (545 m) before arriving at Monte Solaro.

Passetiello The ancient path between Anacapri and the saddle of Capri (or Due Golfi as it's also known locally) has steep sections of crumbly limestone that require great care. This walk is best tackled with a guide, and certainly not for those who suffer from vertigo.

Anginola Like the Passetiello, this path starts near the hospital in Capri, then diverges from it before merging again at the Cetrella church. Giovanni reckons the Anginola trail is safer although there is a tricky section with chains and steel cables that help you hop from ledge to ledge.

Sentiero dei Fortini A coastal path that follows the old forts from the Grotta Azzurra to Punta Carena.

Tragara to Belvedere delle Noci (via Dentecale) This path east of Capri Town takes in heart-pounding coastal views of the Faraglioni rocks, Arco Naturale and limpid blue coves.

the island including a trip to the grotto. Joining the melee of bobbing rowing boats you pay €13 to board one of them and then it's time to duck down while going through the narrow entrance into the cavern beyond. It's usually all over after about five minutes, in which time the oarsmen sing and shout, point at strange rock formations and nudge you for a tip. For the best experience and lighting effects come between 1100 and 1300.

Il Sentiero dei Fortini
Along this stretch of coast there's a fabulous trail, Il Sentiero dei Fortini, that follows the crumbling forts built by Bourbon-backed British troops and enlarged by Napoleonic French after they retook the island in 1808. It passes the scenic ruins of a Roman complex, the Villa Imperiale Romana di Damecuta. Walking guide Luigi Esposito of **Capri Trails** ① *T347-368 1699, capritrails.com*, reckons, "It's best to walk southwards from the Grotta Azzurra to Faro as the sun and sea are in front of you, whereas going the other way you face the cliffs."

Capri listings

For hotel and restaurant price codes and other relevant information, see pages 12-16.

⊖ Where to stay

Capri *p54, map p56*

€€€€ Caesar Augustus, *Via G Orlandi 4, Anacapri, T081- 837 3395, caesaraugustus.com*. Within walking distance of Anacapri, 'Cesare Augusto' – as the locals call it – is perched on cliffs, giving it the most spectacular views across the bay. A sprawling lounge with comfy sofas and piano bar looks onto the long terrace where a statue of Emperor Augustus watches the ferry and yacht traffic. Amid its citrus trees and flowers there's an infinity pool, spa and two restaurants. A secluded mini terrace is laid out for candlelit meals served by your own butler. A shuttle service is available to the port and the Piazzetta.

€€€€ J.K. Place, *Via Prov. Marina Grande 225, near Marina Grande, T081-838 4001, jkcapri.com*. Capri's first quality inn – the Hotel Continental – was housed in this whitewashed 19th-century palazzo. A penthouse and roof terrace have been added as well as all manner of luxuries including two pools (indoor and outdoor), spa facilities, stylish interiors filled with artworks and a sundeck.

€€€ Casa Mariantonia, *Via G Orlandi 180, Anacapri, T081- 837 2923, casamariantonia. com*. Expect beautifully tiled rooms, spacious suites and apartments with terraces overlooking a lemon grove where a Russian revolutionary allegedly laced his *limone* with vodka. Breakfasts are a little basic but overall this is a gem of a place and the Canale family are charming hosts.

€€€ La Minerva, *Via Occhio Marino 8, Capri Town, T081 837 7067, laminervacapri.com*. Top-notch customer service, bright rooms and a tranquil garden setting make this a fine choice near the Capri Town *passeggiata* and Punta Tragara.

€€ Stella Maris, *Via Roma 27, Capri Town, T081-837 0452, albergostellamaris@libero.it*. Up the tiled steps of this *pensione*, opposite the bus station, is a cozy B&B that has been run by the same family for over 25 years now. Expect kitsch decor in the charming lobby-cum-lounge-cum-breakfast room, which hasn't changed much since the late 1980s. The owners have a few apartments dotted around town. Avoid the rooms at the front unless you enjoy the sights and smells of Capri's cute buses.

€€ Hotel Weber Ambassador, *Via Marina Piccola 118, Marina Piccola, T081-837 0141, info@hotelweber.com*. Many rooms here look out over Marina Piccola's pebbly beaches, restaurants and shapely rocks. Rooms have tiled floors and some have small terraces with sea views. A shuttle service takes guests to and from the Piazzetta. Table tennis, mountain biking, fishing and various watersports are on offer.

€ Hotel La Tosca, *Via D Birago 5, Capri Town, T081-837 0989, h.tosca@capri.it*. La Tosca is ensconced down a quiet lane and is a short swagger from the Piazzetta. Breakfasts are taken on the flower-filled terrace with views of the Faraglioni rocks. The clean, simple decor throughout extends to the 11 whitewashed guest rooms with their smallish bathrooms.

Self-catering

Renting an apartment or villa on Capri starts at about €100 per night off-season for two to four people. A useful list of places to stay can be found at capri.com, which includes small apartments such as **Caprihouse** (T328-152 8750, caprihouse.it) and **Casa Malua** (T081-837 9577, casamalua.it).

⊘ Restaurants

Capri *p54, map p56*

€€€€ Torre Saracena, *Via Marina Piccola, T081-837 0646. Apr-Oct daily 1200-1500,*

Sat 1900-2300. The freshest of seafood – plucked from the day's catch tanks – served on the shore. Favourites include *pezzogna all'acqua pazza* (bream cooked in 'crazy' boiling water) and *zuppa di pesce con scorfano* (fish soup with scorpion fish).

€€€ Da Gioia, *Marina Piccola, T081-837 7702. May-Oct daily 1200-1500, 1900-2300, rest of year times vary*. The magical essence of Caprese dining can be found on this boardwalk platform overlooking the Marina Piccola shoreline. The Mennillo family's simple Neapolitan classics like *spaghetti ai frutti di mare* (spaghetti with shellfish), pizza and salads, washed down with a Peroni or wine, hit the epicurean spot best when outside, looking over the sea and towards the Fariglioni rocks. Reservations recommended.

€€€ Da Paolino, *Via Palazzo a Mare 11, T081-837 6102. Thu-Tue 1230-1500, 1900-2400*. Down a leafy lane on the way to Bagni di Tiberio, amid lemon groves and stray cats, is legendary Paolino's, famed for simply prepared seafood dishes such as *totano con patate* – a special, seasonal type of squid served with potatoes.

€€ Il Solitario, *Via G Orlandi 96, 80071 Anacapri, T081-837 1382, trattoriailsolitario.it. Daily 1200-1500, 1900-2400*. Under a pergola near the Santa Sofia church, charming Alessandra and Massimiliano carry on the family tradition started in 1960 when Il Solitario was a tavern for locals. Expect excellent pizzas (try their *pizza bianca*) and wonderful dishes like *calamari alla griglia* (grilled squid), cheese-dream filled *ravioli capresi* and their special *scialatelli pasta* (with some potato in the mix) *alle vongole*. Polish it off with home-made tiramisù.

€€ La Rondinella, *Via G Orlandi 295, 80071 Anacapri, T081-837 1223. Daily 1200-1500, 1900-2300*. The Rondinella combines flavoursome food, relaxed dining and friendly service down the quiet end of Anacapri's main lane. There's a smallish but wonderful terrace (book it!) and a large dining room. The freshest seafood goes into dishes like *linguine al scampo* and *frittura di gambero e calamaro* (fried prawns and squid).

Cafés and bars

Bar Buchetto, *Via G Orlandi 38, Anacapri. Daily 0800-2200*. Near the bus terminal, ever-reliable Bar Buchetto, with charming Michele Scarpato at the helm (70-odd years in the job), delivers *pizza al taglio*, ice cream and refreshments.

Caffè Michelangelo, *Via Trieste e Trento 1, Anacapri. Daily 0800 till late*. The amiable bar staff at this swish bar serve aperitivi with *taralli di finocchietto* (savoury biscuits with fennel seeds) on the terrace while you watch the Anacapresi and tourists go by.

Pasticceria Buonocore, *Vittorio Emanuele 35, Capri Town, T081-837 7826. Daily 0730-2100*. The sweet smell of Buonocore's ice cream cones stays long in the olfactory memory. Its sweet and savoury treats, like lemon-and-almond *caprilù* biscuits and freshly prepared panini, are great for snacks and picnics.

Pulalli Wine Bar, *4 Piazza Umberto I, Capri Town. Closed Tue*. Up near the clocktower is an intimate terrace bar with views over the piazzetta serving drinks, nibbles and excellent dishes.

Sfizi di Pane, *Via le Botteghe 4, Capri Town, T081-837 0106. Tue-Sun 0700-1330, 1600-2000*. Breaded treats including olive breads, cute and crusty rolls (*bacetti*) and *taralli* biscuits make this a good stop for snacks.

⚡ Entertainment

Capri *p54, map p56*
Clubs
Anema e Core, *Via Sella Orta 39/e, Capri Town, T081-837 6461, anemaecore.com. Thu-Sat 2100 till late*. The cheesiest Caprese night club, where Italian celebrities go cheek to cheek and dressed-up locals quaff cocktails, grin and gyrate to live Italo-latino music, including resident crooner Guido Lembo.

Lanterna Verde, *Via G Orlandi 1, Anacapri, T081-837 1427. Thu-Sat 2200 till late.* Piano-bar Italian tunes, rock outfits and live latino sway young and ageing hips at Hotel San Michele's chic nightspot.

⊛ Festivals and events

Capri *p54, map p56*
Procession of San Costanzo, *Capri Town, 14 May.* According to legend, Capri's patron saint and protector was washed ashore here on his way back to Constantinople. A colourful procession to Marina Grande sees Capresi shower the garlanded statue with rose petals.
Procession of Sant' Antonio, *Anacapri, 13 Jun.* Anacapri's saintly protector is honoured with a colourful ceremony involving lots of flower petals and eating of sweets, followed by a concert in piazza Diaz.
Santa Maria del Soccorso, *Villa Jovis, 7-8 Sep.* The ancient church at Villa Jovis is lit up on the evening of 7 September and the following morning a mass is held in honour of the Virgin Mary. Music making, dancing and feasting follow.
Settembrata Anacaprese, *Anacapri, late Aug to early Sep.* The town's four *quartieri* (districts) pit their wits against each other in gastronomic and other quirky contests.

⊙ Shopping

Capri *p54, map p56*
Ceramics
Cose di Capri, *Via G Orlandi 50/a, Anacapri, T081-838 2111.* Interesting ceramics in unusual colours and shapes made by Vittoria Staiano.

Clothing
Canfora, *Via Camerelle 3, Capri Town, T081-837 0487.* Historic Canfora makes quality leather sandals in lots of colours.
100% Capri, *Via Fuorlovado 27-44, Capri Town, T081-837 7561.* Quality luxuries such

as fine cotton beach robes and scented candles fill this oh-so-white outlet.

Food and drink
Fairly cheap, basic picnic ingredients can be gathered at **Supermarket Al** (via Pagliaro 19, Capri Town, and Anacapri) and **Deco** (via Matermania 1, Capri Town). **La Capannina Più**, *Via le Botteghe 39, Capri Town, T081-837 8899.* The posh restaurant's *enoteca* and gourmet shop has lots of wines and food for that very special picnic.
Limoncello di Capri, *Via Roma 79, Capri Town, T081-837 5561; via Capodimonte 27, Anacapri, T081-837 2927.* Many places claim to have invented the syrupy *digestivo*, but the story that this family's first brew oiled the constitution of Russian revolutionary guests is hard not to like.

Perfumery
Carthusia Profumi, *Via Camerelle 10, Capri Town, T081-837 0368; via Capodimonte 26, Anacapri, T081-837 3668.* Carthusia does famous scents – first created by monks and made from the fruit and flora of Capri – and gorgeous packaging.

⊙ What to do

Capri *p54, map p56*
Boat trips
Gruppo Motoscafisti, *Via Provinciale Marina Grande 282, T081-837 7714/5648, motoscafisticapri.com.* Capri must be experienced from the sea. Pack a picnic and hire a boat or join one of the many boat trips offered by the Società Cooperativa Motoscafisti – their distinctive wooden kiosk and fleet can be found at Marina Grande. Classic excursions include tours of the island, through the Fariglione di Mezzo and into the the Grotta Verde, from €35 for a two-hour trip.
Giovanni Aprea, *T347-475 7277 (mobile), aprea.it.* Giovanni Aprea takes groups around Capri's bays and grottoes in his

mildly souped-up Sorrentine *gozzo* sailing boat from €40.

Diving
Sercomor, *C. Colombo 64, Marina Grande, T081-837 8781, T328-721 2920 (mobile), caprisub.com*. Scuba-diving courses and boat tours around Capri.

Sports
Capri Sporting Club, *Via G Orlandi 10, Anacapri, T081-837 2612, caprisportingclub. net*. Tennis courts and *calcetto* (five-a-side) footie pitches in a spectacular setting.

Walking
Capri Trails, *T081-837 5933, T3473-681699 (mobile), capritrails.com*. Luigi Esposito takes walking tours, kayaking adventures and climbing on the cliffs near Faro (€30 per hour, €180 per day).

Wellbeing
Capri Palace, *Via Capodimonte 14, Anacapri, T081-978 0505, capripalace.com. Mar-Nov 0900-1300, 1600-2000*. Specialist medical spa and beauty treatments in the most luxurious surroundings.

⊖ Transport

Capri *p54, map p56*
Capri is just 6 km by 3 km and traffic is restricted so forget about using a car. Ferries from Naples and elswhere arrive at Marina Grande. To reach Capri Town take the 3-minute funicular ride (€1.80) or hop on a bus. Getting around on the tiny orange buses run by **SIPPC** (T081-937 0420) and **Staiano Autotrasporti** (T081-837 1544) is fun and exhilarating as you hurtle around hairpin bends and contemplate dizzying chasms. There are frequent services between Marina Grande, Capri Town, Marina Piccola, Anacapri, Damecuta, Faro, and the Grott'Azzurra; prices from €1.80 for a single bus ride to €8.40 for a day pass allowing unlimited bus travel and 2 funicular rides. Taxis (Capri T081-837 0543, Anacapri T081-837 1175) are very pricey, especially the open-topped vintage vehicles.

Ferries, TMVs and hydrofoils go to Naples, Ischia, Positano, Sorrento and Salerno. Journey times 35-80 minutes. Seasonal timetables apply.

❶ Directory

Capri *p54, map p56*
Money **Banca di Roma**, piazza Umberto I 19, Capri Town, T081-837 5942 (ATM). **Medical services** **ASL Na 5 Guardia Medica**, piazza Umberto I 1, Capri Town, T081-837 5716. **Farmacia Internazionale**, via Roma 24, Capri Town, T081-837 0485. **Post office** Via Roma 50, Capri Town, T081-837 5829 (Mon-Fri 0800-1630, Sat 0800-1230). **Tourist information** **AASCT Capri**, piazzetta Cerio, Capri Town, T081-837 5308, capritourism.com.

Ischia

Ischia's dead volcanoes, steamy thermal fissures and curvaceous craters are evidence of its Campi Flegrei caldera origins. Follow in the sandal-steps of Greeks, Romans and today's ubiquitous German holidaymakers at one of Ischia's popular spa resorts. There are 67 fumaroles (volcanic vents) and a hundred-plus thermal springs across the island, and the island's longest and most coveted stretch of volcanic sand, La Spiaggia dei Maronti is dotted with them. Away from the swanky spas and bulging bathrobes are hilltop villages and exotic gardens sheltered by the shapely tufa-rock topped Mont Epomeo, an extinct volcano reachable on foot or donkey.

Ischia Porto and Ischia Ponte → *For listings, see pages 68-71.*

A volcanic crater was transformed into the island's main harbour, Ischia Porto, by Bourbon King Ferdinand II in 1854. The Riva Destra, along its right bank is lined with yachts and fishing boats, and popular bars and restaurants spill out onto the pitted flagstones of its quayside. Ischia's main shopping drag (via Pontano, corso Vittoria Colonna and then via Roma), known as *il corso* by the locals, connects the port with the medieval town Ischia Ponte via a 228-m-long causeway. A few sandy beaches lie to the east: Spiaggia dei Pescatori, Lido d'Ischia and the public beach, Spiaggia San Pietro e della Marina. Ischia Ponte's fortifications were first laid down in the fifth century BC and today's structure is due to the House of Aragon, hence the name Castello Aragonese.

Castello di Ischia
ⓘ Piazzale Aragonese, Ischia Ponte, T081-992 834, castellodischia.it. Mar-Oct 0930-1700, €10.
The first fortress here was built by Syracusan Greeks in 474 BC and the present towering citadel and bridge (more like a causeway these days) was begun by Alfonso of Aragon in the 1440s. Attacked by Romans, Arabs, Normans, Swabians, French and English, it was not only the strategic stronghold of the island but also a vital place of refuge for the locals. A fairytale romance is also attached to the castle: in the 1500s it became the home of the poet-princess Vittoria Colonna, who married Ferrante d'Avalos here then later became the platonic sweetheart of Michelangelo. Amid its maze of stone steps and higgledy-piggledy structures, there are atmospheric churches, spaces with art exhibitions and some creepy corners. The **Convento delle Clarisse** has the macabre sight of a ring of stone seating, where nuns were laid to rest and decompose, the fluids collected in vases beneath before their skeletons joined their sisters in the Ossarium. Other highlights of the citadel are the museum of torture instruments and the tall 15th-century tunnel.

Museo del Mare
ⓘ Palazzo dell'Orologio, via Giovanni da Procida 3, Ischia Ponte, T081-981124, museodelmareischia.it. Apr-Jun 1030-1230, 1500-1900, Jul-Aug 1030-1230, 1830-2200, Nov-Mar 1030-1230, closed Feb, €4.
Approaching the Aragonese citadel you come to the attractive Palazzo dell'Orologio which houses the Museum of the Sea. The engaging collection is awash with maritime curios, nautical instruments, fishermen's tackle, marine creatures, Marconi's radio equipment and intriguing archaeological finds.

Torre di Michelangelo and Baia di Cartaromana
ⓘ Torre di Guevara, via Nuova Cartaromana, T081-333 1146. Tue-Sun, times vary, free.
The fine sands of the Cartaromana Bay have thermal spring waters and are backed by a rectangular tower, the Torre di Guevara, also known as Michelangelo's Tower. The story goes that Michelangelo stayed here and had a relationship with the poetess Vittoria Collana, who resided in the Aragonese castle over the water, spawning the romantic myth that a secret tunnel connecting the two castles enabled hush-hush rendezvous. The tower is now a cultural centre with occasional art shows.

Around the island

Casamicciola Terme

This popular spa resort 6 km northwest of Ischia Porto is renowned for its 85°C iodine-rich springs. Inventive Iron Age inhabitants tapped into the area's vulcanism for cooking and pottery. In 1883 an earthquake decimated the village. The European aristocracy flocked to its spas on piazza Bagni in the 18th and 19th centuries and many offer state-of-the-art facilities today. Casamicciola Terme's beaches – dell'Eliporto, del Convento and by the Marina – may have some fine grains of sand but they can get mighty busy in the summer and are not the island's most picturesque.

Lacco Ameno

More laid-back than Casamicciola Terme, Lacco Ameno has the most naturally radioactive waters in Italy, with alleged curative powers. The first colony of Neapolitan Magna Graecia was established here at Monte Vico before one too many earth tremors persuaded them to set sail to nearby Cumae and Megaride. The sleepy fishing village was transformed in the 1950s into an exclusive spa resort. Among its famous spa establishments today are the Hotel Regina Elisabetta on piazza Santa Restituta and the exclusive Negombo resort just out of town. Lacco Ameno's logo is the mushroom-shaped volcanic rock offshore, known as *il fungo*.

The local archaeological museum, **Museo Civico Archeologico di Pithecusae** ①️ *corso Angelo Rizzoli, T081-900356, Tue-Sun 0930-1300, 1600-2000, €5, free with Artecard*, is housed in the 18th-century Villa Arbusto. It contains Roman tombs, geological exhibits and archaeological finds including the Coppa di Nestore (Nestor's Cup), a terracotta *kotyle* made in 700 BC on Rhodes and found in the tomb of a child in 1995. Further reminders of Lacco Ameno's past can be found in the **Sanctuary and Church of Santa Restituta** ①️ *piazza Santa Restituta 1, T081-980706*. Next to the pink-hued church is a museum with archaeological finds (don't miss the Egyptian amulets in the form of beetles) and subterranean Graeco-Roman ruins.

Giardini La Mortella

①️ *Località Zaro, T081-986220, lamortella.it. Apr-Oct Tue, Thu, Sat, Sun 0900-1900, €12 plus concessions. Take the SS Forio–Lacco Ameno, towards Chiaia.*

The brainchild of garden architect Russell Page and Susana Walton, the Argentinian widow of English composer William Walton, La Mortella offers a dreamlike garden experience, with fountains, lily ponds, zen water features and subtropical species that thrive in this microclimate beneath the lava flows of Monte Zaro. Pavilions, temples and a tea room add contemplative English and Eastern atmospheres. Check online for details of their programme of Spring and Autumn chamber recitals and Summer Festival of Youth Orchestras.

Forio

The port and town of Forio, on Ischia's western coast, has traditionally been the island's home of winemaking and fishing. From the 1950s to 1970s it became an enclave for artistic types like poet Pablo Neruda and writer-directors Luchino Visconti and Pier Paolo Pasolini. Germans especially enjoy its scenic ramparts and towers. The rotund watchtower that dominates the Forio skyline is home to the **Museo Civico** ①️ *via del Torrione, T081-333*

Where to stay 🛏
1 Albergo della Regina Isabella
2 Aragona Palace
3 Camping Mirage
4 Continental Mare
5 Europa
6 Il Monastero
7 Parco Smeraldo Terme
8 Pera di Basso
9 Villa Caruso
10 Villa Olivia
11 Villa Serena

Restaurants 🍴
1 Al Triangolo
2 Bar Ciccio
3 Bar Pasticceria Calise
4 Mezzanotte
5 Neptunus
6 Umberto a Mare

2934, with exhibits relating to Neapolitan song, artworks (lots by landscapist local hero Giovanni Maltese) and temporary exhibitions.

The elegantly outlined **Santuario della Madonna del Soccorso** ① *via del Soccorso*, is a whitewashed church with majolica-tiled flourishes. Its terrace is the perfect place to watch the setting sun. To the north is the picturesque Spiaggia di San Francesco, with its coarse sand, and beyond it the rocky promontory Punta Caruso. Long and scruffy (but popular) Spiaggia Citara lies to the south of the town, backed by the beach-front gardens of the **Parco Termale Giardini di Poseidon** ① *T081-907122*, one of the most attractive spas.

Panza, Sant'Angelo and Lido di Maronti
Panza, with its restaurants, roadside bustle and joyously yellow San Leonardo church runs into Sant'Angelo, the island's most appealing village, which looks over a harbour with a mound-like islet connected by a sandy isthmus. It's a sublime place to saunter, shop, eat alfresco and visit the beach Lido di Maronti, reached by water taxi in five minutes. This 2-km-long stretch of beach formed from volcanic sand and studded with steaming fumaroles, has some relaxing bar-restaurants. Close to this *spiaggia calda* (hot beach) is the Roman spa resort of Cava Scura. For a tad more exertion trek to Ischia's highest point, Monte Epomeo, for a scramble over smooth tufa rocks and gasp at some stunning views.

For hotel and restaurant price codes and other relevant information, see pages 12-16.

🛏 Where to stay

Ischia *p64, map p67*

€€€€ Albergo della Regina Isabella, *Piazza Santa Restituta 1, Lacco Ameno, T081-994322, reginaisabella.it.* Set up by the legendary film producer Angelo Rizzoli, this luxury hotel retains some 1950s lustre. Spacious suites have terraces overlooking shore-side pools. Spa facilities and treatments are excellent, but not quite up there with Terme Manzi, see page 70.

€€€ Aragona Palace Hotel, *Via Porto 12, Ischia Porto, T081-333 1229, hotelaragona. it.* Comfort and location – it's right on the Riva Destra with its harbourside restaurants – make this a popular choice. Many of the spacious, blue-tiled rooms have terraces with harbour views. Facilities include a smart spa offering treatments.

€€€ Hotel Parco Smeraldo Terme, *Spiaggia dei Maronti, Barano d'Ischia, T081-990127, hotelparcosmeraldo.com.* The bright, cheery and airy hotel is well situated on Maronti beach and many of the 64 rooms have sea views and balconies. Relax in the hotel's subtropical gardens or its wellness centre (with two pools and spa treatments) or hit some balls on the tennis court. Most beach facilities are included and there's a choice of restaurants along the volcanic sands.

€€ Albergo Il Monastero, *Castello Aragonese, Ischia Ponte, T081-992435, albergoilmonastero.it.* Atmosphere and stylish understated interiors make this hotel, housed in the former Convent of Santa Maria della Consolazione within the Castello Aragonese, a special place to stay. Room 21 has a balcony with stunning views of the Chiesa dell'Immacolata and beyond. Their café also serves delicious pastries and looks over the Baia di Sant' Anna.

€€ Hotel Continental Mare, *Via B Cossa 25, Ischia, T081-982577, continentalmare.it.* Whitewashed walls and tiles throughout give this sprawling clifftop hotel a clean fresh feel. Head waiter Luigi is the embodiment of efficiency. There are two pools –a thermal pool within the leafy grounds and a larger pool on an upper terrace. Down some stone steps is a pebbly beach, which alas is not ideal for swimming. Most rooms have small outdoor terraces. Spa treatments are offered at their sister hotel, Continental Terme.

€ Hotel Europa, *Via A Sogliuzzo 25, Ischia Ponte, T081-991427, hoteleuropaischia. it.* The Europa has been run by the same family since the 1950s and is near to Ischia Ponte's historic quarter and Ischia Porto's restaurants, with lots of shops in between. There are 34 reasonably priced rooms with tiled floors and unfussy decor. The hotel provides a thermal pool and spa treatments and organizes excursions and boat trips.

€ Villa Serena, *Via Calata S Antonio 8, Casamiciola Terme, T081-994738, httphotelvillasirena.it.* A solid budget choice with spa pools, colourful tiles aplenty and a homely restaurant. Warm hospitality and green, quiet surroundings.

Camping

Camping Mirage, *Spiaggia dei Maronti, Barano d'Ischia, T081-990551, campingmirage.it. €26 for a small tent and 2 people.* This typically dusty Italian campsite is right next to Maronti beach and has the usual campsite basics including washing facilities and a no-frills bar-restaurant.

Self-catering

Pera di Basso, *Via Pera di Basso (loc. Rarone), T081-900122, peradibasso.it.* Deep in the woods above Casamicciola Terme, this stone farm building has comfortable accommodation and offers tranquillity and outdoor pursuits including trekking and mountain biking. The suite for two costs from €130 per night half-board. The most basic studio apartment at **Villa Olivia** (via Baiola 129, Forio, T081-998426, villaolivia.it), which has gardens and two pools, starts at €350 per week for two people, with various options for different-sized parties. At the other end of the scale is the luxurious **Villa Caruso** (Ville in Italia, T055-412058, villeinitalia.com/houses/PuntaCaruso.jsp), in Forio, which sleeps up to 18, will set you back over €12,000 for a week.

🍴 Restaurants

Ischia *p64, map p67*

€€€ Umberto a Mare, *Via Soccorso 2, Forio, T081-997171, umbertoamare.it. Tue-Sun 1200-1530, 1930-2300.* Sophisticated dining and spellbinding views of the Soccorso shoreline make this a special restaurant. Innovative dishes like local *ricciola* fish with sweet artichokes, fresh basil and lemon can be accompanied by an impressive range of wines. Phone to book a table near the window to enjoy the sunset.

€€ Mezzanotte, *Via Porto 72, 80077 Ischia Porto, T081-981653. Daily 1200-1500, 1900 till late.* A youthful throng spills out onto the Riva at weekends here and there's a cocktail bar upstairs. Expect classic seafood dishes like *spaghetti alle vongole* and a choice of pizzas.

€€ Neptunus, *Via delle Rose 11, Sant'Angelo, T081-999702. Daily 1200-1500, 1930-2400.* Eating the freshest seafood on the terrace here, overlooking Sant'Angelo, is an archetypal Ischian experience. Start with the seafood salad of squid and octopus, squeeze your lemon wedge and let Giuseppe Jacono and team guide you through the menu – it may just climax with a sugar, alcohol and caffeine-

combined rush of *torta caprese*, grappa andva shot of espresso.

Cafés and bars

Bar Ciccio, *Via Porto 1, Ischia Porto. Daily 0700-2200.* Open for over a hundred years, Bar Ciccio does interesting ice-cream flavours including healthy options such as organic, fat-free, doppio-zero and gluten-free.

Bar Pasticceria Calise, *Via Sogliuzzo 69, Ischia Porto, T081-991270.* Sweet filled *cornetti* including the devilish *alla crema e amarene* (with cream and sour cherries) are just some of the pastries enjoyed at this popular spot.

Al Triangolo, *Via Roma, Lacco Ameno, T081-099 4364. Daily 0700-2200.* Near Il Fungo, this is the place for refreshing *granite* in classic and crazy flavours like lemon, melon, coffee, strawberry and yoghurt.

🎵 Entertainment

Ischia *p64, map p67*
Clubs

L'Ecstasy, *Piazzetta dei Pini 3, Ischia Porto, T081-992653. Daily 2000 till late.* A bar-*discoteca* that hosts club nights and live music including jazz acts during September's Jazz Festival.

New Valentino, *Corso Vittoria Colonna 97, Ischia Porto, T081-982569, valentinoischia.eu. Daily 2100 till late.* A bizarre mix of majolica tiling and lurid lighting is the backdrop to wild nights of piano bar and dance music.

✳ Festivals and events

Ischia *p64, map p67*
Festa di Sant' Anna, *26 Jul.* The island's patron saint is honoured with a lively procession of boats, fireworks and feasting around the Castello Aragonese.
Ischia Film Festival, *ischiafilmfestival.it.* Each June Ischia hosts a two-week film festival dedicated to film locations.

🛍 Shopping

Ischia *p64, map p67*
Ceramics
Di Meglio, *Via Roma 42, Ischia Porto,
T081-991176*. A large space brimming with
colourful ceramic plates and tiles.

Food and drink
Ischia Sapori, *Via R Gianturco 2, Ischia
Porto, T081-984482*. Gastronomic goodies,
including liqueurs, olive oils, wines,
handmade pasta and preserves.
Salumeria Manzi, *Via Roma 16, Lacco
Ameno*. With lots of reasonably priced
bread, cheese, meats and fruit and
vegetables, this is a good place to buy
picnic or self-catering provisions.

Souvenirs
Napoli Mania, *Il Corso, Ischia Porto,
napolimania.com*. Novelties in Neapolitan
dialect that many Italians don't understand:
from T-shirts and mugs to baby bibs and
Maradona-related items.

🏃 What to do

Ischia *p64, map p67*
Adventure sports
Indiana Park Pineta, *Loc. Fiaiano, Barano,
T0773-474473. Apr-Oct*. Six colour-coded
arboreal assault courses (they call it)
allow anyone over 110 cm in height to
experience adrenaline-fuelled 'tarzanning',
which involves lots of climbing, swinging
and abseiling around this forest park.

Fishing
Fishing trips with local fishermen from
Ischia Porto and other harbours make for a
magical morning on the waves. **Hotel Tre
Sorelle** (*T081-907792 hoteltresorelleischia.
it*) organizes regular forays at Succhivo.

Sailing
Scuola Vela Ischia, *Hotel Villa Carolina,
Forio, T081-997119, scuolavelaischia.it*.

Sailing school in Forio with courses starting
at €100 for two outings.

Walking
Ischia Trekking, *T368-335 0074 (mobile),
ischiatrekking.it*. Guided treks exploring
the caves of Pizzi Bianchi, Piano Liguori
and Mont' Epomeo (four hours) from €15
per person.

Wellbeing
Parco Termale Castiglione, *Via
Castiglione 62, Casamicciola Terme, T081-
982551, termecastiglione.it*. Historic spa
now with luxurious spaces and outdoor
pools. A day ticket costs €27 and entitles
use of thermal pools, sauna, sunbeds and
changing facilities.
Spa Resort Negombo, *Baia San Montano,
T081-986152, negombo.it*. Arguably Ischia's
most beautiful spa resort, frequented by
both minted megalomaniacs and everyday
Giuseppes. Massage treatments involving
the use of hot healing stones start at €85.
Terme Manzi, *Piazza Bagni, Casamicciola
Terme, T081-994722, termemanzihotel.
com*. Amid the chic interiors, mood
lighting and techie spa equipment is the
tub a wounded Giuseppe Garibaldi sat
in when convalescing during his 1862
Risorgimento campaign. A pricey yet
serene and stylish spa.

🚌 Transport

Ischia *p64, map p67*
Ferries from Naples (21 km), Pozzuoli
(11 km) and elsewhere arrive at Porto
d'Ischia. A system of 19 bus routes run by
SEPSA (*T081-991 1808*) circles the island
in clockwise and anticlockwise directions:
the CD (Circolare Destra) goes clockwise
and the CS (Circolare Sinistra) goes
anticlockwise. Unico Ischia tickets (€1.40)
allow 90 minutes of travel. If you are here
for over a week, car hire is an option.
Companies include: **Di Meglio** (*T081-
995222, ischia-rentacar.it*) and **Mazzella**

(T081-991141, mazzellarent.it). To see the island in comfort contact Giuseppe Lauro (T339-4052691, ischiataxiservice.com).

❶ Directory

Ischia *p64*
Money Banca Monte dei Paschi di Siena, via Sogliuzzo 44, T081-982310. **Medical services Guardia Medica**, T081-983499/ 998989. **Farmacia Internazionale**, via de Luca Alfredo 117, T081-333 1275. **Post office** Via Morgioni, Porto d'Ischia, T081-507 4611 (Mon-Fri 0800-1630, Sat 0800-1230). **Tourist information** AACST **Ischia**, via Sogliuzzo72, Ischia, T081-507 4211, infoischiaprocida.it.

Procida

Located between Capo Miseno and Ischia, Procida is under 4 km long and has a paint-peeling, down-to-earth charm. Its old fishing villages of dishevelled pastel-painted buildings have become a favourite film backdrop, most famously in *Il Postino* and *The Talented Mr Ripley*. Don't expect tourist hordes and glitz here – although its 11,000 inhabitants and summer influx do create traffic mayhem in its centre. There are leafy lanes with attractive villas and market gardens to explore, and the island's fishing tradition lives on, making dining here a treat. Procida's circular bays Corricella and Chiaiolella are dead volcanic craters created by the Phlegrean caldera system, between which are some fine but scruffy beaches.

On arrival at Marina Grande (Porto Sancio Cattolico or, as the locals call it, Sent' Cò) you are greeted by an expanse of sticky, uneven flagstones hosting the usual Neapolitan traffic chaos backed by a ramshackle row of high, pastel-coloured former fishermen's dwellings. The eye-catching arches of these via Roma buildings, under which fishing boats used to be stored, are now occupied by bars and restaurants. Ischia's high street, via Principe Umberto, leads to piazza dei Martiri where the Baroque **Chiesa della Madonna delle Grazie** stands alongside a memorial to 12 Procidani – Republican martyrs killed during a Royalist backlash to a 1799 uprising.

Terra Murata ('walled land'), the highest point on the island at 91 m, offers wonderful views of the fishing port, Marina di Corricella, and beyond. The medieval quarter Terra Casata and the *cittadella* Castello d'Avolos have atmosphere aplenty: the latter was a castle turned Aragonese-built prison (1560s). Nearby the impressive noble residence Palazzo de Iorio has a belvedere with more views.

Abbazia di San Michele Arcangelo
① *Via Terra Murata, T081-896 7612, abbaziasanmichele.it. Daily 1000-1245, 1500-1730, closed Sun and Mon afternoon, church free, museum €3.*
This abbey deep in the Terra Murata was originally built in the 11th century and was repeatedly ransacked by Saracen pirates in the 16th and 18th centuries. Contrasting with the uplifting artistic highs of the exquisite inlaid marble altar, coffered ceiling and flourishes of gold leaf are some macabre sights in the catacombs.

Marina della Corricella, Marina di Chiaiolella and Isola di Vivara
The pastel-coloured buildings and alleyways of Marina della Corricella were the backdrop of the film *Il Postino*, starring the late Massimo Troisi, a Neapolitan comedy genius. Marina Chiaiolella is a crescent-shaped harbour, and also has a fair catch of fishing-harbour lure, with some swanky yachts and bar-restaurants to boot. Another curvaceous crater ridge forms the **Isola di Vivara** ① *accessed via a bridge; permission needed to enter: T081-896 7400, isoladivivara.it,* an island nature reserve with a 109-m-high lump of Mediterranean scrub teeming with birdlife and other animals.

Procida beaches
Although often littered with plastic flotsam and jetsam, Procida's beaches have their charms and lie in stunning positions:

La Spiaggia del Ciraccio Procida's longest and most popular beach is a continuation of Spiaggia della Chiaiolella and just around the corner from Marina di Chiaiolella, on the western shore. Afternoon breezes are welcomed by its sun-worshippers and windsurfers.

Spiaggia della Silurenza Just west of Marina Grande, with ample beach facilities and restaurants. Locals fire themselves off Il Cannone (named after an old cannon placed on the rocks).

Spiaggia della Lingua East of the port, off piazza della Marina Grande, is this intimate beach with limpid waters, popular with swimmers, snorkellers and fishermen.

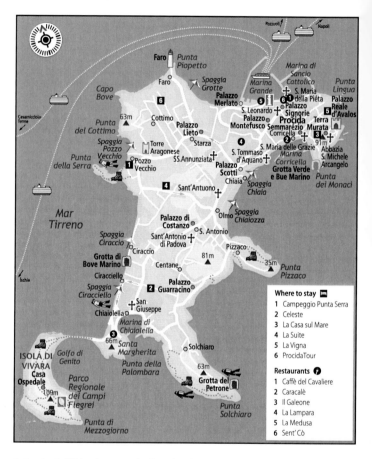

Spiaggia di Chiaia Access to this busy beach's dark coarse sands on Procida's eastern shore involves a descent down 200 steps off piazza San Giacomo, or a boat ride.

Spiaggia Pozzo Vecchio In the northwestern corner of the island (reached from via Battisti) is the Pozzo Vecchio beach, which appeared in *Il Postino* – it is enclosed within a semicircular bay, making it popular with swimmers.

Procida listings

For hotel and restaurant price codes and other relevant information, see pages 12-16.

😐 Where to stay

Procida *p72, map p74*

€€€ La Vigna, *Via Principessa Margherita 46, T081-896 0469, albergolavigna.it.* The crenellated parapet of La Vigna's red-hued tower pokes above the vines in its clifftop vineyard setting. Atmosphere, tranquillity and luxury reign at this *castellino* in the country, a 10-minute walk from the harbour; you can quaff their vino, indulge in therapeutic baths and massages and revel in the effortless style of the place. For those fancying a splurge, the Malvasia suite has a luxury bath set within exotic wood.

€€ Hotel La Casa sul Mare, *Via Salita Castello 13, T081-896 8799, lacasa sulmare. it.* Deep in the Terra Murata historic quarter, this 18th-century residence has 10 elegant rooms decked out in cool hues and tiled floors. Many have small balconies with views. As it sits on a hill, some muscle is required to get around, although a handy beach shuttle service is provided.

€€ La Suite, *Via Flavio Gioia 81, T081-810 1564.* New boutique hotel with whitewashed, minimalist rooms and spacious suites with sea and garden views. There's a spa, pool, bar and access to the beach made famous in *Il Postino*.

€ Hotel Celeste, *Via Rivoli 6, T081-896 7488, hotelceleste.it.* Basic accommodation near Marina di Chiaiolella. Many of the 35 rooms have a balcony or terrace.

Camping

Campeggio Punta Serra, *Via Serra 4, T081-896 9519, campeggioserra@simail.it. Open Jun-Sep.* Pozzo Vecchio beach, granular star of *Il Postino*, is a short walk from this campsite which has pitches for tents and caravans and bungalows for rent (sleeps 2-6, €65-170 per night).

Self-catering

ProcidaTour, *Via Santo Ianno 20, T081-896 9393. procidatour.it.* This family-run enterprise rents out a number of apartments and studios in the Collinetta di Cottimo area. Punto Faro and Pozzo Vecchio beaches are nearby.

🍴 Restaurants

Procida *p72, map p74*

€€€ La Medusa, *Via Roma 116, Marina Grande, T081-896 7481. Daily 1200-1500, 1900-2300.* An idiosyncratic owner and excellent seafood dishes including *spaghetti ai ricci di mare* (sea urchin sauce) make this a memorable place to dine. If the *padrone* (main man) takes a liking to you expect copious amounts of charm and *cibo* (food).

€€ Caracalè, *Via Marina Corricella 62, Corricella, T081-896 9192. Daily 1200-1500, 1900-2300.* Caracalè serves seafood creations like swordfish with aubergine and is a fine spot for absorbing the picturesque Corricella harbour scene. The laid-back atmosphere and unfussy preparation of the freshest catch make it the most beguiling eatery on the *banchina* (quayside).

€€ La Lampara, *Via Marina Corricella, 88, T081-896 0609.* Wonderful terrace restaurant overlooking Marina di Corricella. Tasty marinated seafood antipasti and spicy clams followed by lampara-caught octopus and whatever's in the net.

€€ Sent' Cò, *Via Roma 167, Marina Grande, T081-810 1120. Tue-Sun 1200-1500, 1900-2300.* Sent' Cò is a no-frills ristorante-pizzeria serving the catch of the day and a popular fish soup. Also worth trying are the *orecchiette* (small ear-shaped pasta) with a sauce made from the island's vegetables.

Cafés and bars

Caffè dal Cavaliere, *Via Roma 42, Marina Grande, T081-810 1074. Daily 0700-2100.* Famed for their creamy pastries – *lingue di* *bue* (cow's tongues) – containing Procida's mightily pithy lemons.

Il Galeone, *Via Marina Chiaiolella, Marina di Chiaiolella, T081-896 9622. Daily 0800-2400.* A largish café-bar-restaurant by the harbour serving drinks, pizzas, snacks like *bruschette*, as well as meat dishes and grilled fish.

🎭 Entertainment

Procida *p72, map p74*
GM Bar, *Via Roma 117, Marina Grande, T081-896 7560, gmbar.it. Thu-Sat 2200 till late.* According to the locals this bar-*discoteca* is '*il boom*' at the moment – and it's certainly popular with the young Procidiani who cram in here at weekends for live music, DJs and free buffet food.

🎉 Festivals and events

Procida *p72, map p74*
Procida's festivals include **Festa della Madonna delle Grazie** (2 July), a colourful religious procession with much feasting; **Sagra del Mare** (Festival of the Sea) in late July; **Sagra del Pesce Azzurro** (mid-August), a fish festival in Corricella involving lots of eating and drinking; and **Sagra del Vino** (November), Procida's wine festival.

Good Friday procession. Dating back to 1627, this Easter procession was inspired by the Spanish tradition of the mysteries. Representations of Christ's suffering made by local children are displayed and then a dozen white-robed locals haul an 18th-century wooden statue of the dead Christ to Terra Murata. A funereal procession takes place the following morning.

🛍 Shopping

Procida *p72, map p74*
Food and drink
Il Ghiottone di Imputato M, *Via Vittorio Emanuele 15, T081-896 0349.* Gastronomic

establishment – great for gifts and all you need for a lavish Procidiano picnic.

Souvenirs
Izzo Rosana, *Via Vittorio Emanuele 36, T081-896 9118.* Funky stationery and knick-knacks.

⚓ What to do

Procida *p72, map p74*
De Sanctis, *Via G da Procida, Procida, T081-896 7571.* Tennis and *calcetto* (five-a-side) facilities, best booked for the cool evenings.

⊖ Transport

Procida *p72, map p74*
Boat services from Naples and Pozzuoli arrive at Marina Grande. The island is so small that you can get around on foot, but there are times when you'll need some wheels to take the strain. Four bus routes run by **SEPSA** (T081-542 9965, sepsa.it) cover just about all the island. Walking is not pleasant after dark, especially as there are no pavements, and often piles of rubbish on the roadside. Taxis and microtaxis are pretty cheap and cycling around the quieter lanes can be fun. At Marina Grande there's a taxi rank (T081-896 8785), and nearby you can hire scooters and bicycles from **Ricambio Giuseppe** (via Roma 107, T081-896 0060).

ⓘ Directory

Procida *p72, map p74*
Money Banco di Napoli, via V Emanuele 158, T081-810 1489. **Medical services** Guardia Medica, T081-983499. **Farmacia Madonna Delle Grazie**, piazza dei Martiri 1, Corricella, T081-896 8883. **Post office** Via Libertà 34, T081-896 0711. **Tourist information** Ufficio di Turismo, via Roma, Marina Grande, T081-810968, infoischiaprocida.it.

Contents

78 Ercolano and Vesuvius
- 79 Herculaneum
- 80 *Map: Herculaneum*
- 83 Parco Nazionale del Vesuvio
- 85 Listings

88 Pompeii and around
- 89 Pompeii
- 91 *Map: Pompeii*
- 94 Modern Pompeii
- 96 Listings

Footprint features

81 Five of the best mosaics in Herculaneum

Vesuvius, Herculaneum & Pompeii

Ercolano and Vesuvius

You can squeeze two stupefying sights and a whole lot of history and geology into a day here. In AD 79 the good, the bad and the scholarly (most Romans were squat and ugly according to the Ercolano guides) of Herculaneum were seared by the instant karma of a 482°C pyroclastic surge that roared down Vesuvius at 400 kph. The depth and heat of the blistering debris that swept into the elegant resort helped preserve organic matter including wooden beams supporting roofs, papyrus scrolls of Greek wisdom, and boats filled with the skeletons of those fleeing for their lives. Herculaneum's intimate scale means you need only a few hours to see the wonders of this Roman time capsule.

Grand Tourists were carried to Vesuvius's summit on sedan chairs or aboard the famous funicular railway, whereas today you are now more likely to use less stylish transport to reach the lip of the volcano. Scientists estimate there to be 400 sq km of molten rock 8 km under the well-monitored volcano, and the authorities reassure Neapolitans that there should be ample warning to evacuate the 600,000 people living in the Zona Rossa (Red Zone) nearest the volcano. Imagine living on the slopes with the threat of a Plinian eruption: in 2007 some scientists controversially posited that an event like the cataclysmic Avellino eruption 3780 years ago is not out of the question.

Herculaneum → *For listings, see pages 85-87.*

ⓘ *Ercolano scavi (Herculaneum excavations), corso Resina, Ercolano, information T081-857 5347, ticket office T081-777 7008, pompeiisites.org. Apr-Oct daily 0830-1930, Nov-Mar daily 0830-1700, last entry 90 mins before closing time, closed 1 Jan, 1 May, 25 Dec. €11, €5.50 18-25, free under 18/over 65. Audioguide €7, €4 for children. You can visit all five archaeological sites – Herculaneum, Pompeii, Oplontis, Stabiae and Boscoreale – within three days by buying a biglietto cumulativo (combined ticket) for €20, €10 18-25, free under 18. The entrance to the site is a 5-min walk downhill from Ercolano station.*

Herculaneum was a well-to-do Roman town of around 5000 residents, with elegant seaside villas, many of which were buried to a depth of over 15 m by the huge pyroclastic flows of the AD 79 eruption. In 1709 Emmanuel de Lorraine, Prince d'Elbeuf, came across the back of the Roman theatre while digging a well and shortly afterwards the first haphazard excavations began. The nature of the volcanic deluge resulted in fewer roofs collapsing here than in Pompeii, and the searing heat carbonized organic materials, meaning that extraordinary architectural details, bodies and objects are still being discovered. Around 300 skeletons were found huddled together in boathouses along with fine jewellery in the 1980s, and it's reckoned that archaeologists have only brushed the surface of the so-called Villa dei Papiri (see page 82) and its fascinating library of Graeco-Roman scrolls. Indeed some hope that papyri will be revealed containing the lost works of Greek writers such as Epicurus, Aristotle and Euripides.

The broad sloping path that curves around and descends into the archaeological site allows you to appreciate the enormity of the AD 79 eruption and the vast amount of debris that buried the town. It also provides an overview of the Roman grid layout of the streets and blocks. The roads orientated north-south are the *cardi* while the east-west routes are called *decumani*. These define the six rectangular *caseggiati* (blocks or sections) of the city, known as *insulae*.

Insulae II and III

The first building on Cardo III Inferiore is the **Casa di Aristide** (House of Aristides) where fleeing victims' skeletons were found. One of Herculaneum's finest villas (discovered in 1828) is next door, the **Casa d'Argo** (House of Argus), named after a painting depicting the myth of Argus, which sadly was stolen. Opposite is the back entrance to the **Casa dell'Albergo** (House of the Inn), not an inn at all but a sprawling villa that was undergoing refurbishment at the time of the eruption. The only private *thermae* (thermal baths) were found here, while a carbonized pear tree trunk was found in the garden.

No prizes for guessing what was found in the **Casa dello Scheletro** (House of the Skeleton). The less palatial **Casa dell'Erma di Bronzo** (House of the Bronze Herm) has a bronze sculpture of the owner and a Tuscan-style atrium. On Cardo IV the **Casa del Tramezzo di Legno** (House of the Wooden Partition) is a grand Roman dwelling named after the wooden partition that closes the *tablinium* (main room). Seek out the mosaic paving, corniced façade and dog's-head spouts on the compluviate roof that channels rainwater to a sunken pool. There were shops, including one used by a *lanarius* (fabric maker), known as the Bottega del Lanarius (Store with a Clothes Press) – you can see the instrument inside.

Insulae IV and V

You get a feel for the might of tectonic forces at work when you see the geometric mosaic flooring rippled by the eruption in the **Casa dell'Atrio a Mosaico** (House of the Mosaic

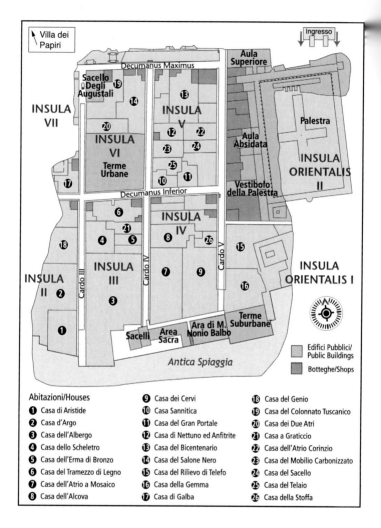

Abitazioni/Houses

1. Casa di Aristide
2. Casa d'Argo
3. Casa dell'Albergo
4. Casa dello Scheletro
5. Casa dell'Erma di Bronzo
6. Casa del Tramezzo di Legno
7. Casa dell'Atrio a Mosaico
8. Casa dell'Alcova
9. Casa dei Cervi
10. Casa Sannitica
11. Casa del Gran Portale
12. Casa di Nettuno ed Anfitrite
13. Casa del Bicentenario
14. Casa del Salone Nero
15. Casa del Rilievo di Telefo
16. Casa della Gemma
17. Casa di Galba
18. Casa del Genio
19. Casa del Colonnato Tuscanico
20. Casa dei Due Atri
21. Casa a Graticcio
22. Casa dell'Atrio Corinzio
23. Casa del Mobilio Carbonizzato
24. Casa del Sacello
25. Casa del Telaio
26. Casa della Stoffa

Atrium). Next door, the **Casa dell'Alcova** (House of the Alcove) has a lavish room with paintings and wooden couches.

The **Casa dei Cervi** (House of the Deer) was an opulent waterfront residence named after two marble groups of deer being savaged by dogs in the garden (the originals are in the Archaeological Museum in Naples). A drunken Hercules relieves himself nearby.

The **Casa Sannitica** (Samnite House) has the layout of a pre-Roman dwelling, with an imposing portal of Corinthian capitals and a graceful open gallery with Ionic columns and fabulous frescoes. Just as grand is the elegant façade of neighbouring **Casa del**

Five of the best mosaics in Herculaneum

Terme Urbane Disrobing females and flies on the steamy walls of the *apodyterium* (changing room) would have got an eyeful looking down at the floor in the Public Baths: floating centre stage is the mermaid-like Greek god Triton wielding a trident in one hand and clasping a fish in the other, while a naughty cherub is ready with a whip. A maelstrom of maritime beasts, including dolphins, a cuttlefish and an octopus, whirl around.

Casa di Nettuno ed Anfitrite Head to the *triclinium* (a kind of summer dining room/ lounge) for a look at vibrant glass paste mosaic designs studded with seashells. On the east wall stands a languid-looking Neptune, the god of water and the sea, grasping his triton alongside his scantily clad queen Amphitrite, who leans on a plinth. On the north wall a nymphaneum (fountain and shrine) has similarly vivid tiles depicting dogs chasing deer amid garlands of fruit, flowers and birds. The niche would have held statues and fountains fed by a tank set into the wall.

Palaestra Mosaic swimmers and an anchor motif once shimmered beneath the water of the gymnasium pool. Although now accessed by cool tunnels excavated from the massive pyroclastic debris (look at the layers and depth!) from the AD 79 eruption, the large alfresco cross-shaped pool here was surrounded by a grandiose colonnade.

Casa dell'Atrio a Mosaico The rippled geometric designs in the House of the Mosaic Atrium reveal the full force of the AD 79 eruption – the combination of meandering lines and mysterious motifs in the entrance followed by an expanse of chequerboard design buckled by seismic forces strikes an alluring yet unsettling note. Over wavy floors you are led into a grand space with pillars resembling a basilica – this is the Egyptian **oecus** (reception room) that the Roman architectural writer Vetruvius described as being all the rage with nobles wanting to wow their tight curly big-wig guests.

Villa dei Papiri Archaeologists await further funding and the go-ahead to discover yet more geometric-patterned mosaics and crazy paving in this most exquisite 'casa delle Muse': House of the Muses.

Gran Portale (House of the Great Portal) with its two pilasters, demi-columns and carved capitals with winged Greek-style Victories.

Under the **Casa di Nettuno ed Anfitrite** (House of Neptune and Amphitrite) is a well-preserved wine store with intact wooden fittings, counter and shelves for amphorae. Along the east wall is the remarkably vivid Neptune and Amphitrite glass wall mosaic. The much-photographed *nymphaeum* has elaborate decoration depicting hunting scenes and attractive motifs, all topped with a head of Silenus (best mate of wine god Dionysus). On the *decumanus maximus* is the **Casa del Bicentenario** (House of the Bicentenary), found in 1938 by top archaeologist Amedeo Maiuri, 200 years after Charles III began the official digs.

Insula VI

The **Terme Urbane** (Thermal Baths) date back to the first century AD, during the reign of Augustus. Separate baths and entrances for men and women are on Cardi III and IV respectively. Unusual red and black interiors mark out the **Casa del Salone Nero** (House of the Black Hall). Worth checking out are the two large panels depicting Jupiter, Hercules, Juno, Minerva and the Etruscan god Acheloo in the **Sacello degli Augusti** (College of the Augustali), the seat of the cult of Emperor Augustus.

Insulae Orientalis I and II

Head eastwards to the **Palaestra**, the public sports centre, with its monumental vestibule, a lower terrace with porticoes, a long pool for breeding fish and part of a cruciform swimming pool. Seek out the mythical five-headed serpent, Hydra, entwined around a tree trunk. The 18th-century Bourbon excavation tunnels run beneath the avenue here, offering an insight into the scale of the excavations.

Moving to the SE corner of the excavations is three-storey **Casa del Rilievo di Telefo** (House of the Relief of the Telephus), Herculaneum's largest villa, named after a bas-relief depicting the myth of Telephus – the son of the god Hercules – founder of the city. Don't overlook the circular plaster cast copies of the original marble *oscilla* (discs depicting satyrs to ward off evil) hung between the red-hued columns. Also on Cardo V is the **Casa della Gemma** (House of the Gem), named after an engraved stone found here, where there are large frescoed panels and refined graffiti in the toilets recording the visit of a renowned physician.

Suburban district

On the western fringes of the south terrace are the **Sacelli** (Sacred areas) which have two temples – one dedicated to Venus and the other to four gods: Neptune, Minerva, Mercury and – most fittingly – Vulcan. The **Terme Suburbane** (Suburban Baths) has a *frigidarium* with white marble flooring and a *tepidarium* with a stuccoed wall depicting warriors. There's an extraordinary impression made by a *labrum* (washing tub) on the volcanic material that immersed the *caldarium*. Nearby is a half disrobed and handless statue of the senator M Nonius Balbus, an ally of Octavian (who reigned as Augustus from 27 BC to AD 14).

A theatre is buried nearby accessed via 18th-century tunnels dug by Prince d'Elbeuf's speculative excavators – its *scaenae frons* (monumental stage backdrop) was unceremoniously stripped of its lavish decoration and statuary. This area was right on the beach: boat storehouses and warehouses line the old shoreline. In the early 1980s, 300 human skeletons and then a 9-m-long Roman boat containing an oarsman, soldier, swords and a pouch of coins were found here. In 2008 work began on recreating the beach.

Villa dei Papiri

ⓘ *Northwest of main excavation. The villa is currently not open to the public.*

Historians believe that this most opulent villa, where a priceless library of papyrus scrolls was discovered, belonged to Lucius Calpurnius Piso Caesoninus, father-in-law of Julius Caesar. In the 1750s engineers dug into the multi-storey villa when excavating a well. The scale and beauty of the residence is mind-blowing: covering almost 3000 sq m, the villa had a 250-m-long shoreline frontage, rooms filled with exquisite art and statuary, a porticoed garden and terraced grounds brimming with vineyards, orchards and fountains. The Archaeological Museum in Naples houses a collection of marble and bronze busts from the villa.

Museo Archeologico Virtuale (MAV)

ⓘ *Via IV Novembre, Ercolano, T081-1980 6511, museomav.com. Tue-Sun 0900-1830, €7.50, €5 for 3D virtual show, €11.50 combined.*

Opened in July 2008, this €10 million museum near the ruins takes visitors on a virtual journey around the villas and public spaces of ancient Herculaneum. There are lots of interactive multimedia displays to explore as well as some intriguing sights, smells and temperature fluctuations thrown in to get you into the Roman mood. A new immersive 3D show, *Eruption of Vesuvius*, allows you to imagine the force of the eruption.

Ville Vesuviane including Villa Campolieto

ⓘ *Corso Resina 283, Ercolano, T081-732 2134/081-192 44532, villevesuviane.net. Tue-Sun 1000-1300, free, a 5-min walk heading east from the entrance to Herculaneum.*

In the 1700s, sumptuous aristocratic residences were built along the coast from San Giovanni a Teduccio to Torre Annunziata. The celebrated stretch of road from Resina to Torre del Greco known as the *Miglio d'Oro* (Golden Mile) has many a classical pile but alas most are privately owned or in disrepair. Collectively they are known as as the Ville Vesuviane. In Ercolano you can visit the Villa Campolieto, home of the Ente per le Ville Vesuviane that overlooks the restoration and preservation of these mansions – 122 of them – and organizes guided tours, by appointment, of many villas including Villa Favorita. Opportunities to hobnob with the Bourbon descendants are best during the annual events: *Emozioni Vesuviane* (late April to June), the *Festival delle Ville Vesuviane* (when classical concerts are held at mansions built by the likes of Vaccaro and Vanvitelli) and *Natale nelle Ville* at Christmas. The Royal palace **Reggia di Portici** ⓘ *via Università 100, Portici, T081-775 5109*, and its Villa d'Elbeuf by Sanfelice are also open by appointment.

Parco Nazionale del Vesuvio → *For listings, see pages 85-87.*

ⓘ *Park headquarters Ente Parco Nazionale del Vesuvio, piazza Municipio 880040, San Sebastiano al Vesuvio, T081-771 0911, vesuviopark.it; visitor centre at summit T081-777 5720/ T081-739 1123. For those wanting to combine visits to Pompeii and Vesuvius in a day, City Sighteesing Napoli/Eavbus run a bus service (T081-551 3109, unicocampania.it, €10 return). Compagnia Trasporti Vesuviani has a small office outside Ercolano Scavi station and runs regular minibuses (often cramped, so don't bring luggage) to the National Park car park for €12 return or €17 including entrance to the volcano. The minibus departs for the volcano when full and waits for about an hour at the car park, so there's not that long to enjoy the visit. The park path is open daily from 0900 and closing times vary throughout the year – last admission is about 90 mins before sunset. €8, €6 under 18/student, free under 8 accompanied by an adult.*

Summit walk

The route to the summit of Vesuvius involves motor transport to the entrance car park followed by a walk over volcanic rocks. All vehicles, bar the jeeps driven by official guides, stop at the car park at 1017 m. The climb to the summit is around 250 m over rough ground, which combined with the heat of a summer's day or high winds can make for an uncomfortable walk for even the fittest person. The Vesuvius National Park authority looks after the protected area around the volcano and their nature trail (No 5 of nine routes, see page 84) incorporates part of the ascent to the summit and halfway around the crater. Upon reaching the visitors' centre you pay an admission charge to enter the park and go to the crater's rim.

The views along the steep, wide gravelly path and around the mountain are incredible. Inside the crater (out of bounds unless accompanied by a guide, see page 84) fumaroles steam amid luridly coloured rock crystals and silver-grey pumice. The 200-m chasm to the floor of the crater adds to the dizzying spectacle. A rusty, makeshift handwritten sign points the way to Pompeii down below. A souvenir stall-cum-bar sells assorted tat, snacks, postcards, refreshments and Lacryma Christi wine.

Osservatorio Vesuviano
① *Via Diocleziano 328, T081-610 8483, ov.ingv.it. Sat-Sun 0900-1400, free.*
Built by Bourbon monarch Ferdinand II in the 1840s, the neoclassical Vesuvian Observatory has an exhibition exploring volcanology, with lots of video, observatory instruments and interesting collections of volcanic rock. Eyes are fixed nervously on the instruments that record the seismic and geochemical activity across 300 sq km – they are monitored closely from the surveillance centre in Fuorigrotta.

Adventure trips within the park
Adventurous types will relish a trek in the otherworldly volcanic landscape of Vesuvius National Park or a scramble into the crater itself, accompanied by an expert guide. You can combine a trip to Herculaneum with a trip to the summit, perhaps followed by a trek along one of the designated trails around the park. Sturdy walking boots with ankle support, outdoor kit (from mid-October to May especially) and food supplies are essential.

Into the crater with vulcanologist Roberto Addeo Special guided tours can be taken from the visitor centre with the likes of amiable Guida Vulcanologica, Roberto Addeo. Roberto explains that the general public are prohibited from going beyond the perimeter fence into the crater unattended as there have been some fatalities over the years: "People have gone down into the crater and have become asphyxiated by the noxious fumes." While experienced personnel abseil down onto the crater floor to take samples, conduct studies and roll hot rocks, regular punters get the chance of a mini-Vesuvian cocktail of adrenaline and eggy-steamy vapours. After a short and slightly tricky 20-m scramble down the slope of the crater, Roberto encourages me to stick my face into the steamy fumaroles to feel and sniff the sulphurous heat of Vesuvius. Glasses steamed up and knees knocking, I look up and hear a young, breathless English voice above: "Oh my god! What are they doing down there? They are crazy!" Roberto regularly confronts the real dangers lurking beneath our feet: "The only things that remind you that the volcano is active, apart from the fumaroles, are the small earthquakes, which start with a muffled sound and then there are the occasional landslides that fill the crater with dust. In those moments you get a little edgy."

Trekking in Vesuvius National Park ① *For National Park headquarters, visitor centre and transport options to the summit, see page 87. For further information and maps contact the park wardens or official guides, T081-777 5720, T337-942249 (mobile), guidevesuvio.it.*
Within the Vesuvius National Park there are nine colour-coded trails, varying in difficulty. Trail 4 (orange) is a seven-hour round trip and covers over 8 km of rough terrain including the Tirone Alto Forestry Nature Reserve, established in 1972. On the trail you can hear and see lizards, martens, cuckoos, foxes and hares. Trail 9 (grey) *Il Fiume di Lava* (the Lava Flow) is a much easier 90-minute circular track that starts and ends at via Osservatorio. Amid the 1944 lava flows is a unique yellow lichen species, *stereocaulon vesuvianum*, that thrives on mineral-rich magma and whose very mention can set a botanist's heart pounding.

Ercolano and Vesuvius listings

For hotel and restaurant price codes and other relevant information, see pages 12-16.

🛏 Where to stay

Ercolano and Vesuvius *p78*

€€ Bel Vesuvio Inn, *Via Panoramica 40, San Sebastiano al Vesuvio, T081-771 1243, agriturismobelvesuvioinn.it.* This attractive 18th-century farmhouse with modern comforts is set amid vineyards on the slopes of Vesuvius. It's especially good for nature lovers and families as there are farmyard animals, a playground, horse riding, local walking trails and a *bocce* area where you can enjoy Italian boules. Meals are served on a large terrace and feature local produce including *piennolo* tomatoes, apricot jam, cheeses, chicken and *salume.*

€€ Miglio d'Oro Park Hotel, *Corso Resina 296, 80056 Ercolano, T081-739 9999, migliodoroparkhotel.it.* The 18th-century Villa Aprile is within easy reach of Herculaneum, with awe-inspiring views of Vesuvius and a new pool. Its fountains and garden follies reveal the whimsical tastes of its first owner, the Count of Imola and Forlì, Gerolamo Riario Sforza. It's all very modern with some crazy artworks spanning various cubed spaces around a lounge bar. A smart glass and chrome lift whisks you to the guest rooms, which range from a reasonably priced Classic to the spacious Suite – all have fabulous bathrooms (some with jacuzzi baths, others with jet showers), air conditioning, internet and satellite TV.

€€ La Murena B&B, *Via Osservatorio 10, Ercolano, T081-777 9819.* This small B&B is a good base for exploring Vesuvius National Park and visiting the Vesuvian Observatory and Herculaneum. The accommodation includes suites and an apartment with a kitchen and a terrace for alfresco dining, while the wonderful grounds are a great place to eat breakfast and relax. There's

also the option of renting the entire house for €260 per night.

€ Andris Hotel, *Via San Vito 130, Ercolano, T081-777 7220, diiserniagroup.it.* Top-value modern hotel, with helpful staff, simply furnished rooms in a quiet location and bay/Vesuvius views. Great family-option room sleeping four for around €100.

€ Il Cavaliere, *Via Gramsci 109, 80040 Massa di Somma, T081-574 3637, agrodelcavaliere.altervista.org.* From Naples take the SS162, exit at Cercola and follow signs to Massa di Somma. Good value accommodation, an *agriturismo* farmyard, stunning views, a pool and superb food make 'The Knight' a hit with Neapolitan families and couples seeking a rural getaway. Their *casalinga* (homemade cooking) fixed menu (€30) meal starts with an antipasto selection of meats, cheeses, *frittelle* and local vegetables, followed by a pasta dish and barbecued meat. A children's menu is available, and their local white wine is made with an old variety of Catalan grape, *l'uva catalanesca.*

🍴 Restaurants

Ercolano and Vesuvius *p78*

€€€ Casa Rossa al Vesuvio, *Via Vesuvio 30, Ercolano, T081-777 9763. Wed-Mon 1230-1500, 1900-2300.* The sister restaurant of the renowned Casa Rossa 1888 in Torre del Greco, the Pink House is all about elegant Neapolitan dining. The house specialities include Parthenopean pasta dishes like *vermicelli ai frutti di mare* and *paccheri al ragù di mare.* They also do pizza and have a selection of the very best Lacryma Christi del Vesuvio wine.

€€€ Viva lo Re, *Corso Resina 261, Ercolano, T081-739 0207, vivalore.it. Tue-Sat 0930-0100, Sun 0930-1600.* This cozy osteria-enoteca run by serenely suave Maurizio Focone has handsome wooden interiors lined with hundreds of bottles of wine. Some may find the presentation of the food a tad pretentious (it comes on fancy flat, angular plates) but the food itself is expertly prepared. *Piatti del giorno* are written on a board and often include a plate of *pesce crudo* (raw seafood), grilled cuttlefish with bitterly delicious *friarelli* (a type of broccoli and an acquired taste) and chunky steaks. They also have three stylish rooms overlooking Villa Campolieto.

€€ La Lanterna, *Via Colonnello Aliperta 8, Somma Vesuviana, T081-899 1843. Tue-Sun 1200-1500, 1930-2300.* After a day on the slopes of Vesuvius, vulcanologist guide Roberto Addeo enjoys coming here to try their various *baccalà* dishes: the imported Norwegian stockfish (*stucco* or *stoccafisso*) is a traditional ingredient in Somma Vesuviana cuisine. Their classic pasta dish is the much imitated *paccheri con lo stucco* and they also make pizzas including *pizza al baccalà*, which is best eaten outside under the garden pergola.

€ Il Cavaliere, *Via Gramsci 109, 80040 Massa di Somma, T081-574 3637. Sat-Thu 1200-1500, 1930-2300.* Booking is essential at this popular *agriturismo* known for its excellent cooking – see page 85.

Cafés and bars
L'Angolo degli Scavi, *Via IV Novembre 1, Ercolano. Daily 0730- 2100.* Just over the road from the Scavi entrance, on the 'Corner of the Excavations', this small and often busy bar is convenient but the prices are geared to tourists. You are better off walking further up via IV Novembre to one of the many bars used by the locals.

🎭 Entertainment

Ercolano and Vesuvius *p78*
Sciuscià Club, *Via Viulio 2, Ercolano, T081-771 9898, sciusciaclub.it.* Commercial house music and latino pumps out under the vaulted ceilings, and there's a garden where you can sample Neapolitan classics. Check in advance for latest programme.

🛍 Shopping

Ercolano and Vesuvius *p78*
Food and drink
F/lli de Luca Bossa, *Via IV Novembre 4/6, Ercolano. Daily 0800-1300, 1600-2100.* This tiny *alimentari* near the entrance to the Scavi is where the locals come for their supplies. As well as decent bread and snacks like *taralli di finochietto*, you can pick up a bottle of Valdobbiadene prosecco for just €6 and a large bottle of water for €1 here.

Markets
Mercato di Resina, *Piazza Pugliano, Ercolano. Daily 0730-1300.* Famous since the Second World War, when impoverished locals peddled objects and clothes stolen from the Allied forces, colourful Resina second-hand market often throws up a quirky clothing item. Just take care of con artists offering dodgy electronics goods and cigarettes.

🎯 What to do

Ercolano and Vesuvius *p78*
Cultural
Arethusa, *T0823-448084, arethusa.net.* This company provides group tours all over Italy including guided visits to the archaeological sites around Vesuvius.

Itinera, *Corso Vittorio Emanuele 663, Naples, T081-664545/339-7551747 (mobile), itineranapoli.com. Metro to Corso V. Emanuele.* Friendly, English-speaking Francesca del Vecchio organizes a host of tours along the Bay of Naples including trips around the Vesuvian sights. A two-hour guided tour around Pompeii or Herculanuem costs €130 (for up to four people) while a four-hour tour of Pompeii or Herculanuem, plus Vesuvius, costs €160.

L'Ultima Notte di Ercolano, *T081-8631581, tappetovolante.org. €25 – check for latest programme.* This is a tour under the stars with a theatrical performance thrown in – 40 costumed actors perform Domenico

Maria Corrado's musical version of Virgil's *Aeneid* amid Ercolano's ancient baths and villas.

Walking and outdoor activities
Vesuvio Trekking, *T333-866 4497, vesuviotrekking.com.* Roberto Addeo is one of the vulcanological guides who take people around the Vesuvius National Park. The guided walk around the crater costs €8. Roberto can be contacted on his mobile T338-441 0102 or via email at vesuviotrek@libero.it.
Vesuvio Wild Eco Campus, *Via Cifelli, Trecase, vesuviowild.it, T081-247 4698/T334 170 7752.* Rope work, climbing, mountain biking, geocaching and survival courses organized by outdoor enthusiasts in the Tirone Alto Vesuvio forest.

⊖ Transport

Ercolano and Vesuvius *p78*
Reaching Ercolano by train is easy but ascending Vesuvius is less straightforward: the Eavbus services are the most reliable way. To get there by road take the A3 Napoli–Salerno Autostrada and exit at Ercolano.

Eavbus (T800-053939, eavbus.it) runs various services around Vesuvius and Ercolano, connecting with Naples and satellite towns around the bay. Alternatively take an infrequent public bus or a small minibus outside Ercolano station. Note, however, that these minibuses are cramped and do not allow much time at the summit.

Ercolano's bus station is on piazzale stazione 1. **ANM Autobus** T081-7631111.

By train, From Naples or Sorrento, take the **Ferrovia Circumvesuviana Railway** to Ercolano from the Stazione Vesuviana

(Corso Garibaldi; Metro: Garibaldi); there are stations as far as Sorrento.

Ercolano's train station, **Circumvesuviana Ercolano**, is on piazzale Stazione 1, T800-053939, T081-772 2444, vesuviana.it.

Ercolano Scavi *p79*
Frequent Circumvesuviana train services to Napoli (20 mins), Pompei Scavi (20 mins), Torre Annunziata-Oplonti (15 mins), Castellammare di Stabia (30 mins) and Sorrento (50 mins).

Parco Nazionale del Vesuvio *p83*
Eavbus from Naples – Piazza Garibaldi (65 mins), Pompei – Piazza Anfiteatro (90 mins), Ercolano Circumvesuviana station (35 mins).

❶ Directory

Ercolano and Vesuvius *p78*
Money Banca Monte dei Paschi di Siena, at piazza Longo B40, T081-863 6511. **Medical services Ospedale Maresca**, via Montedoro 2, Torre del Greco, T081-849 0191. **Corso Italia 9**, Ercolano, T081-739 0021 (daily 0900-1300, 1600-2000). **Post office** Via Panoramica 298, Ercolano, T081-739 5385. (Mon-Fri 0800-1330, Sat 0900-1230.) **Tourist information** Via IV Novembre 82, Ercolano, T081-788 1243. For information about Herculaneum, check out pompeiisites. org. **Parco Nazionale del Vesuvio** (Via Palazzo del Principe, Ottaviano, T081-865 3911, parconazionaledelvesuvio.it) has information about the park and guided walks in the area, including night time visits to the crater. Vesuvius Information Point, Contrada Osservatorio, T081-777 8069.

Pompeii and around

Around 20,000 people lived in Pompeii when Vesuvius spewed and spat ash, pumice and wave upon wave of scorching pyroclastic debris on the town in AD 79, sealing a bubble of Roman life for 2000 years. Built on a lava plateau the city was ruled by Oscans, Etruscans and Samnites – Italic tribes – as well as by Greek colonists, before the Roman Empire ceded it. Walking around Pompeian streets, houses, baths and shops among its graffiti, artworks and artefacts of horror is a spellbinding experience that warrants a couple of days' exploration.

Mind-boggling time-travel explorations of AD 79's victims continue at the dreamlike, epicurean gardens of Villa Oplontis, where Nero's colourful second wife Poppaea Sabina sojourned. At Boscoreale, further up the slopes of Vesuvius, visitors can discover life on a Roman farm and vineyard. Four villas were found at Roman Stabiae and more artefacts will be unearthed in the coming years as part of a US$200 million archaeological project.

Shoddy management and millions of visitors (2.6 million visited the ruins at Pompeii in 2007) have taken their toll on the area's ancient treasures; the government has declared a state of emergency with new emphasis placed on protecting the excavations. Bureaucratic inertia and headline-hitting collapses at the House of the Gladiators and Domus di Diomede now threaten Pompeii's UNESCO Patrimony of Humanity status.

Pompeii → *For listings, see pages 96-98.*

ⓘ *Pompei Scavi, via Villa dei Misteri 2, Pompei, information T081-857 5347, ticket office T081-536 5154, pompeiisites.org. Apr-Oct 0830-1930 (last entry 1800), Nov-Mar 0830-1700 (last entry 1530), closed 1 Jan, 1 May, 25 Dec, €11, €5.50 EU citizens 18-24/school teachers, free EU citizens under 18/over 65. You can visit all five archaeological sites – Herculaneum, Pompeii, Oplontis, Stabiae and Boscoreale – within three days by buying a* biglietto cumulativo *(combined ticket) for €20, €10 18-25, free under 18. Porta Marina entrance is just over the road from the Scavi-Villa dei Misteri station.*

Fascination in the beauty and sophistication of Pompeii's everyday objects, buildings and society is tempered with the horror of its devastation. Thousands stayed behind after the first deluge of volcanic debris: some perhaps to save their possessions from looting, some no doubt just unable to flee. Roofs collapsed under the weight of ash and pumice, crushing many before the massive pyroclastic surges engulfed everyone and everything. Haunting casts of human and animal victims created by archaeologist Giuseppe Fiorelli, who poured plaster into cavities left by bodies in the ash, freeze the mortal positions of the incinerated victims.

Pompeii covers 67 ha, 44 ha of which have been excavated. Its walls are punctuated by seven gates: Marina, Ercolano, Vesuvio, Nola, Sarno, Nocera and Stabia. Many of its older Greek-influenced buildings and irregular sixth-century BC street plan are around the Foro Triangolare (Triangular Forum) area. The later grid layout, with rectangular *insulae* (urban blocks), *decumani* (east-west streets) and *cardi* (north-south streets) date from the fourth century BC onwards.

Orientation

The vast scale of the Pompeii ruins makes it worthwhile having a planned route around the site (bear in mind though that some villas may be closed). However, the heat of the sun and stamina will also play a part in your day out – bring lots of sun protection, water and energy-giving snacks. Set out early in the morning if you can and plan a rest for the hottest part of the day in a cool spot – the trees around the amphitheatre provide welcome shade. Expect lots of walking on uneven ancient surfaces, so pace yourself and mind your step.

The description below divides the sprawling 44 ha area into mini-itineraries that roughly follow the classic route from porta Marina, opposite the Circumvesuviana station, ending up at the amphitheatre. To take in all these sights and the suburban villas and baths requires a couple of full days, so pick out the most interesting ones to visit.

Here is a five-hour route that starts at the porta Marina and ends at the amphitheatre: around the Forum, Casa del Fauno, Casa di Vettii, Casa degli Amorini Dorati, Lupanare, Terme Stabiane, the Theatre district, the western section of Via dell' Abbondanza, Palestra Grande and the Anfiteatro.

Forum On entering through Porta Marina you come to the **Tempio di Venere** (Temple of Venus), dedicated to the city of Pompeii's guardian goddess, then the **Basilica**, seat of the law courts, before the Roman **Foro** (Forum) opens out to your left. The Forum was the centre of the city's public life, covering 17,400 sq m and containing governmental buildings and temples.

Starting clockwise, the **Tempio di Apollo** (Temple of Apollo) was erected on the site of an earlier building constructed by the southern Italian Samnites in the fifth century

BC. Seek out the bronze statue of Artemis shooting arrows here. The **Granai del Foro** (the *holitorium* or grainstore) houses archaeological finds and some poignant plastercasts of some of the victims of the AD 79 eruption (other examples can be seen at the Garden of the Fugitives and the Stabian Baths). At the north end, flanked by two triumphal arches, is the *Tempio di Giove* (Temple of Jupiter), which became the Roman Capitolium – the raised podium once had statues of Jupiter, Juno and Minerva.

The Forum is still the meeting place of a motley flock, nowadays consisting of tour parties, snoozing stray dogs and Italian school kids who hop on the empty plinths and strike poses. There is little shade but it's worth lingering here by the patch of grass to view the architectural fragments backdropped by Vesuvius. On the east side you'll find the **Macellum** (market), the **Sacrarium** (more venerated deities) and the **Edificio di Eumachia** (Building of Eumachia), the headquarters of the wool fullers, who cleaned (with a brew of urine and potash) and thickened woollen cloth. Exquisite marble decoration depicts birds and insects amid acanthus leaves here, while the marble altar of the **Tempio di Vespasiano** (Temple of Vespasian) has bas-reliefs of a sacrificed bull. Municipal elections were held at the Comitium.

North of the Forum The **Terme del Foro** (Forum Thermal Baths), built around 80 BC, have rich architectural details including a stuccoed *tepidarium* (warm water baths) and terracotta *telamones* (male figures supporting the ceiling). At the junction of via del Foro and via della Fortuna is the **Tempio della Fortuna Augusta** (Temple of Fortuna Augusta) whose once-magnificent Corinthian columns, double staircase and towering marble-faced entrance were built in honour of an imperial cult by Marcus Tullius, a military man, imperial knight and ally of Augustus.

Towards Porta Ercolano On the way to Porta Ercolano and the suburban villas (which is a fabulous detour for those with extra time and stamina, see page 94) is the area first excavated by archaeologists – it may have consequently faded and been damaged but has a striking atmosphere and views. On via Consolare is the mighty old **Casa di Sallustio** (House of the Sallust) dating from the third century BC. It was split into various commercial uses, becoming an inn with a *thermopolium* (restaurant) after the AD 62 earthquake, and suffered the indignity of a 1943 US air attack. Beyond the grand frontage of *opus quadratum* pillars of tufa stone are cavernous interiors, a clever *viridarium* (garden) with an Ionic portico and a luxuriant *trompe l'œil* garden scene painted on the back wall. The nearby **Casa del Chirurgo** (House of the Surgeon) is a colossal building where grisly looking surgical instruments were found.

Via del Mercurio Starting at the **Torre del Mercurio** (Tower of Mercury) and heading south on via del Mercurio, there are some grandiose dwellings. The **Casa di Apollo** (House of Apollo) has a mosaic of Achilles at Skyros, the **Casa di Meleagro** (House of Meleager) contains a fountain, fish pond and a simple fridge, while the **Casa di Adone** (House of Adonis) is named after a painting of a wounded Adonis tended by Venus and some cupids. The grandest though is the **Casa dei Dioscuri** (House of Castor and Pollux) with its imposing colonnade and mythological paintings of Apollo and Daphne, Adonis and Scylla. Paintings of the Dioscuri, the Divine twins Castor and Pollux, that adorned the entrance, and of Perseus and Andromeda, are in the Archaeological Museum in Naples.

Further along is the **Casa della Fontana Piccola** (House of the Little Fountain), with its *trompe l'œil* effects and a cute cherub grasping a goose, while neighbouring **Casa della**

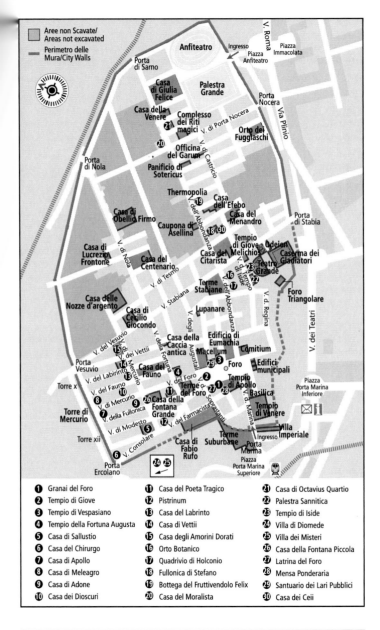

❶	Granai del Foro	⓫	Casa del Poeta Tragico
❷	Tempio di Giove	⓬	Pistrinum
❸	Tempio di Vespasiano	⓭	Casa del Labirinto
❹	Tempio della Fortuna Augusta	⓮	Casa di Vettii
❺	Casa di Sallustio	⓯	Casa degli Amorini Dorati
❻	Casa del Chirurgo	⓰	Orto Botanico
❼	Casa di Apollo	⓱	Quadrivio di Holconio
❽	Casa di Meleagro	⓲	Fullonica di Stefano
❾	Casa di Adone	⓳	Bottega del Fruttivendolo Felix
❿	Casa dei Dioscuri	⓴	Casa del Moralista

㉑	Casa di Octavius Quartio
㉒	Palestra Sannitica
㉓	Tempio di Iside
㉔	Villa di Diomede
㉕	Villa dei Misteri
㉖	Casa della Fontana Piccola
㉗	Latrina del Foro
㉘	Mensa Ponderaria
㉙	Santuario dei Lari Pubblici
㉚	Casa dei Ceii

Fontana Grande (House of the Large Fountain) has a mosaic fountain and tragicomic masks. More mosaics and theatricality fill the **Casa del Poeta Tragico** (House of the Tragic Poet), where a much-reproduced mosaic in the floor of the vestibule warns visitors to '*Cave Canem*' ('Beware of the dog').

House of the Faun Crowds gather around the copy of the statuette of a dancing faun at the **Casa del Fauno** (House of the Faun), a large house covering over 3000 sq m. Its best finds include the *tesserae* mosaic of Alexander the Great tussling with Darius at the Battle of Issus, now at the Archaeological Museum in Naples. Around the corner on vicolo Storto is the best-preserved *pistrinum* (bakery), whose millstones and bulbous ovens were owned by one Popidius Priscus.

Casa di Vettii and around vicolo di Mercurio On vicolo del Labrinto at the **Casa del Labrinto** (House of the Labyrinth) there's a mosaic maze depicting Theseus slaying the Minotaur, while the must-see **Casa di Vettii** (House of the Vetti) has lavish paintings in the Fourth Style (the most intricate decorative style that was all the rage around the time of the AD 62 earthquake), peppered with mythology and mischievousness. Owned by the Vettii family of freedmen, who prospered around the time of the AD 62 earthquake (look out for the electoral slogans on the south wall) and commissioned quality restoration after the quake, it is much visited and consequently damaged by footfall. It has been undergoing restoration in recent years.

The Vettii's conversation pieces include a modestly endowed and demi-proud Priapus, and a witty frieze lined with endearing cherubs (or psyches) busy peddling gold and perfume, lobbing stones at a target and topsy-turvy chariot racing. Look out for the cherub cracking the whip astride a crab. The sumptuous *triclinium* (dining room) and *oecus* (living area) have a compendium of mythology and include lots of romantic couples (Perseus and Andromeda, Dionysius and Ariadne, Poseidon and Amymone) and Hellenistic scenes, including Ixion bound to a spinning wheel, punishment for leering at Zeus's wife. Statues of Bacchus and cupids clutching grapes and a goose were rigged up to a sophisticated system of fountain jets in the *peristyle* (porticoed garden). Other highlights include erotic paintings in the servants' quarters (some scholars guess that it was a private brothel) and the frescoed *lararium* (shrine) with household gods (*lares*) and a snake.

Historians reckon the well-to-do Poppaei family owned the **Casa degli Amorini Dorati** (House of Gilded Cherubs), at the junction with via del Vesuvio, renowned for its marble relief bacchanalian scenes, Egyptian gods and gold cupids.

Around porta di Nola On via di Nola is the extensive **Casa del Centenario** (House of the Centenary), excavated in 1879, 18 centuries after Vesuvius's eruption. A certain A Rustius Verus owned and enjoyed its baths with Egyptian flourishes, a *nymphaeum* and garden fountain portraying a young satyr pouring wine. In the servants' atrium – now in the Archaeological Museum in Naples – was a celebrated scene showing Bacchus with a cape of grapes among birds, snakes, a panther and a vine-strewn Vesuvius.

Eastern section of via dell'Abbondanza Starting at the Forum, Pompeii's wide high street slopes down to porta di Sarno and is lined with shops, workshops and hostelries. The inscriptions along the way offer insights into the commercial, political and sexual lives of the people of Pompeii. Stepping stones would have been handy to hop over water and detritus. Deep ruts attest to the busy cart traffic that would have rumbled along here. Imagine the onslaught of movement, sound and pongs, with Vesuvius brooding in the corner of your left eye.

Terme Stabiane Entering the Stabian Baths, along the via dell'Abbondanza, the men's *tepidarium* is a whirl of intricate stucco work and camera shutters. In the footsteps of ancient bathers, you enter the antechamber (dressing room) with its *clipei* (shields) decorated with nymphs and cupids, then the *tepidarium* and circular *frigidarium* with its plunge pool and twinkling, lapis lazuli dome. The niches held towels and massage ointments. Bathers would then brave the *calidarium*'s 40°C steam and hot baths, followed by a massage in the *tepidarium*. Patrons would relax with a drink under the porticoes of the *palaestra*. According to some scholars, women paid almost double to enter their baths, which are adjacent to the mens' and were accessed on the vicolo del Lupanare.

Side-trip to the Lupanare Expect a lot of eye-bulging images advertising personal services in the compact brothel quarters of the **Lupanare** (named after the howl of a lupa: she-wolf) on the vicolo del Lupanare. Among the tiny cubicles are pieces of Latin graffiti, including: "Long live lovers, death to those who do not know how to love! Double death to those who hinder love!"

Western section of via dell'Abbondanza Upon reaching the **Nuovi Scavi** (new excavations begun in 1911 yet largely untouched to the north), there are a number of small businesses such as the **Fullonica di Stefano** (Stefano's Laundry), **Thermopolia** (inns serving hot food and drink), and the **Bottega del Fruttivendolo Felix** (Shop of Felix the Fruit Merchant), with its amusing Bacchic scenes. There are lots of middle-class dwellings along here. The **Casa del Moralista** (House of the Moralist) has a fine loggia and gardens, and the **Casa di Octavio Quartio** (House of Octavius Quartius) has scenes from *The Iliad* and a long marble pool shaded by a pergola. Don't miss the huge **Casa di Giulia Felice** (Villa of Julia Felix) with its extensive gardens and baths.

Towards porta di Stabia On via Stabia is the main entrance to the sprawling **Casa del Citarista** (House of the Lyre Player), which has a copy of a statue of a wild boar and snarling dogs. Victims were crushed by a shaky peristyle at the **Casa del Menandro** (House of the Menander) along nearby vico Meridionale. It was excavated by celebrated archaeologist Amadeo Maiuri in 1930-31 and is important for its lavish furnishings, decoration and jewellery, including cluster earrings of gold globes and green semi-precious gems strung on golden thread. Don't miss the painting of the poet Menander and exquisite mosaic flooring in the private *thermae* depicting a bunch of acanthus with a bird and sea creatures including dolphins. A rib-tickling multi-coloured mosaic in the *oecus* shows porky pygmies punting along the Nile. It's reckoned that the villa was owned by the magistrate and friend of the Empress Poppaea (who liked a milky bath), Nero's second wife.

Theatre district Hellenistic influences between the sixth and second centuries BC feature in the layout and history of the theatre district. The monumental **Foro Triangulare** (Triangular Forum), with its Ionic portico leading to a Doric colonnade and temple, was a venue for religious and athletics events, while the **Palestra Sannitica** (Samnite Palaestra) had a statue of Doryphorous. The **Tempio di Giove Melichios** (Temple of Jupiter Meilichios) was dedicated to a Greek cult as well as Jupiter, Juno and Minerva. Greek-aping turns into the capers of the Egyptian cult of Isis at the **Tempio di Iside** (Temple of Isis) where small bones were found on the main altar. Picture the scene: shaven-headed priests in black robes and men with dog-faced masks performing weird rituals.

The **Teatro Grande** (Large Theatre) had a two-storey Greek-style *scaenae frons* at the back of the stage, with doorways for the thesps and niches with honorary statues, all framed with entablatures and columns. Next door is the **Odeion** (Odeon), a small covered theatre built around 80 BC. The **Caserma dei Gladiatori** (Gladiatorial Barracks) has the Quadriporticus, a large square surrounded by a portico.

Around the amphitheatre and porta Nocera Welcome shade is provided by the tunnel entrances, porticoes and surrounding trees around the amphitheatre and Great Palaestra. The **Anfiteatro** (Amphitheatre) is an elliptical structure begun around 70 BC and completed around the turn of the new millennium. It's the oldest surviving Roman amphitheatre and an incredible arena to explore, making a fitting climax to a day in Pompeii. Gladiatorial battles were watched by around 20,000 spectators, seated in three tiers, or the *cavea* (sections for different social classes). Roman chronicles and inscriptions found outside the arena, where spectators gathered to eat and chant at the popular inns, attest to the popularity of star gladiators: Felix was the "bear fighter", Thracian Celadus was dubbed "a heart-throb" and Oceanus was the "barmaid's choice". Boisterous rivalry spilled over into hooliganism in AD 59 when Pompeians clashed with rivals from Nuceria. In 1823 tons of volcanic debris was cleared from the site but it was not until the 20th century, under the archaeological eye of Amedeo Maiuri, that it was properly excavated.

The **Palestra Grande** (Great Palaestra) was built under the reign of the state-strengthening Emperor Augustus as a place where the *collegia iuventum* (youngsters) could train body and mind, primarily in preparation for Roman army service. It has a sloping pool that was continually fed water by a lead pipe, and the 141 x 107 m area is enclosed on three sides by a handsome portico. Stucco reliefs found here depict Dionysus as a wrestler and an athlete resting on an exercise hoop. Rows of plane trees have been planted recently to recreate the layout of AD 79.

In 1961 13 victims of the eruption were revealed near the porta Nocera, at the **Orto dei Fuggiaschi** (Garden of the Fugitives).

Suburban villas and baths

Outside the city walls, at Porta Marina, erotic artworks were recently exposed in the **Terme Suburbane** (Suburban Baths). Built in the first century BC, the multi-storey complex was the only unisex baths in Pompeii and probably had a brothel on the top floor. It has mosaics and stuccoed cherubs. Nearby, the **Villa Imperiale** has frescoed rooms splashed in Pompeian red.

The via dei Sepolcri, outside Porta Ercolano, is lined with tombs and leads to two opulent residences. The **Villa di Diomede** (Villa of Diomedes) had the largest garden in Pompeii. During the excavations in the late 1700s, 18 skeletons of unlucky souls who tried to escape were found in the vaulted cellar. The **Villa dei Misteri** (Villa of Mysteries) has a colourful history: this sumptuous pile was turned into a large winery but it's the Dionysian Cycle in the so-called Hall of Mysteries – nine scenes from a ritual dedicated to the Greek god of wine and revelry, Dionysus – that really captures the imagination. Although outlawed by Rome, the cult thrived further south in this Hellenistic region and perhaps explains some of those exuberant Neapolitan traits.

Modern Pompeii

Modern Pompeii has nondescript shopping streets fanning out from piazza B Longo, which has four patches of grass interspersed with a fountain, palm trees and benches.

The focal point is the impressively flamboyant pilgrimage shrine dedicated to the Madonna of the Rosary, **Santuario della Madonna del Rosario** ① *Piazza B Longo 1, T081-857 7111, santuario.it, May-Oct daily 0900-1300, 1530-1830, Nov-Apr Mon-Fri 1500-1700, Sat-Sun 0900-1300, free*), built in the late 19th century. Weekend and festival services are particularly worth attending, when you can inhale much Neapolitan piety and incense amid atmospheric surroundings.

Oplontis – Villa di Poppaea

① *Via Sepolcri, Torre Annunziata, T081-862 1755, pompeiisites.org. Circumvesuviana railway to Torre Annunziata. Turn left at the front of the station and walk for 5 mins.*

Villa di Poppaea is a large and lavish suburban Roman villa at Oplontis, near the port of Torre Annunziata, around 7 km from Pompei and 20 km southeast of Naples. It's reckoned that Nero's second wife Poppaea Sabina lived here. *Trompe l'œil* architectural details and lively landscape scenes filled with birds, butterflies, theatre players and fruits of the land fill the atrium, *triclinium*, *caldarium* and gardens. Bodies, gold jewellery, coins and statues were found crammed in the storeroom, making it likely that the villa was being restored at the time of the AD 79 eruption.

Boscoreale

① *Antiquarium Nazionale Uomo e Ambiente nel Territorio Vesuviano, via Settetermini 15, Località Villaregina, T081-857 5347, pompeiisites.org. Circumvesuviana railway to Boscotrecase, then shuttle bus to Villa Regina.*

Once a rural hamlet and Pompeian suburb, Boscoreale is located to the north of Pompei on the slopes of Vesuvius. It's worth seeking out for its archaeological museum which houses finds from the area's working Roman villas. Exhibits bring the workings of a Roman farm to life and a visit to Villa Regina with its vineyards, *torcularium* (grape press) and wine cellar is a must for vino quaffers. Fabulous frescoes and a hoard of silver were discovered in the 1800s at two nearby villas, the Villa di Pisanella and Villa di Publius Fannius Synistor. Their treasures can be seen in the Archaeological Museum in Naples, the Louvre in Paris and the Metropolitan Museum of Art in New York.

Stabiae (Scavi di Stabia)

① *Via Passeggiata Archeologica, Castellammare di Stabia, T081-871 4541, pompeiisites.org. Circumvesuviana railway to Castellamare or Via Nocera then red No 1 bus.*

Castellammare di Stabia, a spa town with shipbuilding traditions, is 33 km southeast of Naples and marks the start of the Sorrentine Peninsula. Its excavated Roman villas and *antiquarium* (museum) are currently being transformed by one of the largest archaeological projects in Europe since the Second World War. The plan is to create a 60-ha Stabiae archaeological park that will encompass the four villas already discovered at Roman Stabiae, which were excavated in the 18th century and from the 1950s onwards. Named after a wall painting of the mythological Ariadne found asleep by Dionysus, the **Villa di Ariana** ① *via Piana di Varano, T081-274200*, is just outside the modern town at Varano. Nearby is the **Villa di San Marco** ① *via Passeggiata Archeologica, T081-871 4541*, a wealthy residence with frescoes, stucco work and the remains of a swimming pool. The walk is well worth it for the views alone and you may even be lucky to glimpse ancient treasures coming to light.

Pompeii and around listings

For hotel and restaurant price codes and other relevant information, see pages 12-16.

☺ Where to stay

Pompeii and around *p88*

€€€ Crowne Plaza Stabiae, *SS145 Sorrentina, Località Pozzano, 80053 Castellammare di Stabia, T081-394 6700, ichotelsgroup.com.* This former factory building has strangely alluring modernist shapes. Stylish accommodation, a choice of indoor and outdoor pools, and a private beach make this hotel far more glamorous than its industrial origins would suggest. The 157 rooms have clean contemporary lines and some have terraces with stunning views of the bay of Naples. There is one obvious downside: unless you have a car you'll have to rely on the free shuttle bus to Vico Equense and the train station.

€€ Hotel Forum, *Via Roma 99, 80045 Pompei, T081-850 1170, hotelforum.it.* Beyond the recently added contemporary façade, set back from busy via Roma, the Forum offers good value near the piazza Anfiteatro, the modern town and Santuario. The staff in the lobby are friendly and helpful. The best of the 36 guest rooms are in the new wing, which have smart modern bathrooms and better soundproofing than the other rooms. Buffet breakfast is served in a rather scruffy space but fortunately there is a leafy garden.

€€ Hotel Santa Caterina, *Via Vittorio Emanuele 4, Pompei, T081-856 7494, hotelsantacaterinapompei.com.* Conveniently located on via Roma opposite the entrance to the ruins, this pleasant hotel has 20 cosy guest rooms in which Pompeian red hues and classical paintings abound. There are impressive views of either Vesuvius or the amphitheatre from some rooms while another two have been customized for

disabled access. The English-speaking staff are helpful and there's free parking.

€ Hotel Diana, *Vico Sant'Abbondio 10, 80045 Pompei, T081-863 1264, pompeihotel. com.* This modern and well-run hotel is near the Pompei Scavi, Santuario and town amenities. It won an Italian hospitality award in 2007. Expect good service and immaculate, brightly decorated rooms in various sizes to suit most needs, even if the bathrooms are a little on the small size. Facilities include a laundry and dry-cleaning service, while the garden filled with citrus and palm trees is a considerable bonus.

☺ Restaurants

Pompeii and around *p88*

€€€ President, *Piazza Schettino 12, Pompei, T081-850 7245, ristorantepresident. com. Tue-Sun 1200-1500, 1930-2330.* Il President's elegant rooms often host themed evenings with historic culinary creations served from ancient times to the Bourbon era. Their *la cucina povera napoletana extravaganza* sees tiny 17th-century-style Neapolitan pizzas on the menu. They also organize candlelit walks around the ancient city – their website has details of all their latest gastronomic events. Reservations recommended.

€€€ Il Principe, *Piazza Bartolo Longo 8, Pompei, T081-850 5566, ilprincipe.com. Tue-Sat 1200-1500, 1945-2230, Sun 1200-1500.* Ancient Roman recipes with multi-ethnic origins (especially Arabic, African and Greek) dominate the menu at this large restaurant brimming with Pompeian design. Some courses have culinary antecedents from Roman times, including the *garum pompeianum*, a piquant anchovy-based sauce served with pasta. Other inventive creations include *arselle con scampi su timballo di riso selvatico*: clams and scampi with wild rice.

€ **Addu' u Mimi**, *Via Roma 61, Pompei, T081-863 5451. Sat-Thu 1200-1500, 1930-2300.* This is a relaxing place to eat near the centre of modern Pompei, serving good-value food, although service is often charmless and portions are not generous, so you will probably need a few courses. They serve salads and pizzas for veggies and tasty seafood pasta dishes.

Cafés and bars

Caffè Spagnolo, *Via Giuseppe Mazzini 45, Castellammare di Stabia, T081-871 1272. Thu-Tue 0800-2200.* A *stile-Liberty* (Italian art nouveau) gem near Roman Stabiae at Castellammare di Stabia. The surroundings are handsome and everything is top quality, from the coffee and pastries to the focaccia and ice cream.

De Vivo, *Via Roma 36/38, Pompei, T081-863 1163. Daily 0730-2200.* This gelateria-pasticceria on via Roma does savoury snacks including panini, a range of gelati, *sorbetti* and *semifreddi*, as well as sweet creations including *sfogliatelle*, *pastiera* and *Babà al limoncello*.

O Shopping

Pompeii and around *p88*
Food and drink

Melius, *Via Lepanto 156, Pompei. Daily 0800-1300, 1600-2100.* A fabulous deli with homemade meals as well as cheeses and salame to fill your panini bought from the *paneficio* (bakery) next door. Great too for food and wine to take home.

Mirto, *Via Lepanto 142, Pompei. Daily 0830-2000.* A decent supermarket in the modern town which is useful for picnic products and food to take home.

Photographic supplies

Foto Shop, *Via Sacra, Pompei, T081-850 7816.* A handy shop for camera equipment.

O What to do

Pompeii and around *p88*
Cultural

Itinera, *Corso Vittorio Emanuele 663, Naples, T081-664545, itineranapoli.com. Metro to Corso V. Emanuele.* Friendly, English-speaking Francesca del Vecchio organizes trips around the Vesuvian sights.

Ufficio Scavi, *Villa dei Misteri 2, T081-857 5347, pompeiisites.org.* For details about guided tours, themed adventures and latest access to restricted areas around the Scavi, contact this office.

Wellbeing

Terme di Stabia, *Viale delle Terme 3/5, Castellammare di Stabia, 081-391 3111, termedistabia.com. Daily 0900-1900.* Alas concrete and crazy paving covers most of the ancient baths here but the complex does still provide mineral waters with curative properties, a Centro Benessere offering spa beauty treatments and medical programmes for sports injuries.

O Transport

Pompeii and around *p88*

To get here by road, take the A3 Autostrada and exit at Pompei Ovest then follow signs to Pompei Scavi; Torre Annunziata and follow signs for Boscoreale; Torre Annunziata Sud then signs for Scavi di Oplonti; Castellammare di Stabia and the SS145.

SITA (T081-5522176, sitabus.it) runs various buses from piazza Garibaldi in Naples to Pompei and along the Amalfi coast.

By train, from Naples or Sorrento: take the **Ferrovia Circumvesuviana Railway** (T800-053939, vesuviana.it), which departs regularly from the Stazione Vesuviana (Corso Garibaldi; Metro: Garibaldi) and along the coast from the Sorrento station – it stops at Pompei, Boscoreale, Torre

Annunziata-Oplonti Villa di Poppea and Castellammare di Stabia.

The **Circumvesuviana** railway is also the cheapest and most convenient way of getting to and around the archaeological sites.

If you'd prefer to visit the area using a tour guide, **Itinera** (T081-664545, itinera napoli.com) runs tours around the sites.

Pompei Scavi-Villa dei Misteri *p89*
Frequent Circumvesuviana train services to Napoli (35 mins), Torre Annunziata-Oplonti (5 mins), Castellammare di Stabia (10 mins), Ercolano (20 mins) and Sorrento (30 mins).

Torre Annunziata-Oplonti *p95*
Frequent Circumvesuviana train services to Napoli (30 mins), Castellammare di Stabia (15 mins), Pompei (10 mins), Ercolano (20 mins) and Sorrento (35 mins).

Castellammare di Stabia *p95*
Frequent Circumvesuviana train services to Napoli (45 mins), Pompei (10 mins), Torre Annunziata-Oplonti (15 mins), Ercolano (30 mins) and Sorrento (20 mins).

🅞 Directory

Pompeii and around *p88*
Money Banca Monte dei Paschi di Siena at piazza Longo B40, T081-863 6511 (ATM). **Medical services** Hospital Pronto Soccorso, Via Colle San Bartolomeo 50, T081-535 9111. **Farmacia Pompeiana**, via Roma 12, Pompei, T081-850 7264. **Post office** Piazza Esedra 3, T081-5365200 (Mon-Fri 0800-1330, Sat 0800-1230). **Tourist information** Ufficio AASCT, piazza Esedra 12, T081-536 3293.

Contents

100 Index

Footnotes

Index → *Entries in bold refer to maps.*

A

Abbazia di San Michele
    Arcangelo, Procida
    73
accommodation 12-13
    price codes 13
Agerola 36
agriturismi 12
airport 8
air travel 8
Amalfi 37
Amalfi Coast 34-45
    directory 45
    entertainment 43
    restaurants 42
    shopping 43
    transport 45
    what to do 44
    where to stay 41
Anacapri 57
Anfiteatro, Pompeii 94
Atrani 38

B

Bagni di Tiberio, Capri
    57
Bagni Nettuno, Capri 57
Baia di Cartaromana,
    Ischia 65
Baia di Ieranto 28
Belvedere Cannone,
    Capri 55
boat trips 32, 44, 62
Boscoreale 95
bus/coach travel 9, 11

C

Capodanno (New Year)
    16
Capo d'Orso 40

Capri 54-63, **56**
    bathing spots 57
    directory 63
    entertainment 61
    festivals and events
        62
    restaurants 60
    shopping 62
    transport 63
    walks 59
    what to do 62
    where to stay 60
Capri, Ischia and Procida
    53-76
    overview 6
Capri Town 55
car hire 8, 11
Carnevale 16
Casa di Sallustio,
    Pompeii 90
Casa di Vettii, Pompeii
    92
Casamicciola Terme,
    Ischia 66
Castellammare di Stabia
    95
Castello di Arechi,
    Salerno 47
Castello di Ischia, Ischia
    65
Centro Visite Valle delle
    Ferriere 37
Ceramiche Artistiche
    Solimne, Vietri 40
Certosa di San Giacomo,
    Capri 55
Cetara 40
Chiesa di San Benedetto,
    Salerno 47
Chiesa di San Francesco
    d'Assisi, Sorrento 26

Chiesa di Santa Maria
    Assunta, Positano 35
Chiesa di Santissima
    Annunziata, Vico
    Equense 25
Chiesa San Michele
    Anacapri 58
Conca dei Marini 36
Concerti al Tramonto 17
cooking courses 44
cuisine 13-16
customs and
    immigration 19
cycling 11, 44

D

Deserto 28
disabled travellers 19
diving 33, 63
drink 14-16
driving 10
Duomo, Amalfi 37
Duomo di San Filippo e
    San Giacomo,
    Sorrento 26
Duomo di San Lorenzo,
    Scala 37
Duomo di San Matteo,
    Salerno 47
Duomo, Ravello 38

E

Easter 16, 76
emergency numbers 19
Erchie 40
Ercolano 78-87
    directory 87
    entertainment 86
    restaurants 85
    transport 87

what to do 86
where to stay 85
Estate Amalfitana 17
etiquette 19

F
families 19
Ferragosto 17
Ferrovia Circumvesuviana 10
Festa della Madonna del Carmine 17
Festa della Madonna delle Grazie 76
Festa di San Costanzo 16
Festa di San Pantaleone Mass 17
Festa di Santa Lucia 18
Festa di Sant'Andrea 17, 18
Festa di Sant' Anna 69
Festa di Sant'Anna 17
Festa Nazionale della Befana 16
Festa Tradizionale dell'Annunziata 16
festivals 16-18
Fiordo di Crappola 28
fishing 70
food and drink 13-16
Forio, Ischia 66
Furore 36

G
Giardini La Mortella, Ischia 66
Gli Scavi di Paestum 48
Grotta Azzurra, Capri 58
Grotta dello Smeraldo 36

H
health 19
Herculaneum 79-83, **80**
mosaics 81
Suburban district 82
Villa dei Papiri 82
House of the Faun, Pompeii 92

I
Il Salto di Tiberio, Capri 56
Il Sentiero dei Fortini, Capri 59
insurance 19
Ischia 64-71, **67**
directory 71
entertainment 69
festivals and events 69
Ischia Ponte 65
Ischia Porto 65
restaurants 69
shopping 70
transport 70
what to do 70
where to stay 68
Ischia Film Festival 69
Isola di Vivara, Procida 73

L
Lacco Ameno, Ischia 66
Lido di Faro, Capri 57
Lido di Maronti, Ischia 67
Linea d'Ombra 16
Lupanare, Pompeii 93

M
Maggio dei Monumenti 17
Maiori 39
Marina del Cantone 28
Marina della Corricella, Procida 73
Marina della Lobra 27
Marina di Chiaiolella, Procida 73
Marina di Equa, Vico Equense 25
Marina Grande, Procida 73
Marina Piccola, Capri 57
Massa Lubrense 27
Minori 39
money 20
Monte Solaro, Anacapri 58
Museo Antiquarium Equano, Vico Equense 25
Museo Archeologico Nazionale, Paestum 48
Museo Archeologico Virtuale (MAV), Herculaneum 82
Museo Bottega della Tarsia Lignea, Sorrento 26
Museo Civico, Amalfi 37
Museo Correale, Sorrento 27
Museo della Carta, Amalfi 38
Museo del Mare, Ischia 65
Museo Mineralogico Campano, Vico Equense 25
Museo Narrante del Santuario di Hera Argiva, Paestum 49

N
Nerano 28

O
opening hours 20
Oplontis 95
Osservatorio Vesuviano 84

P

Paestum 47
  restaurants 50
  where to stay 50
Pane e Olio in Frantoio 17
Panza, Ischia 67
Parco Nazionale del Vesuvio 83
Piazza Tasso, Sorrento 26
police 20
Pompeii 89-98, **91**
  directory 98
  Modern Pompeii 94
  restaurants 96
  shopping 97
  transport 97
  what to do 97
  where to stay 96
Pontone 36
Porta Ercolano 90
Positano 35
post 21
Praiano 35
Presepi di Natale 18
price codes 13
Processione dei Misteri 16
Procession of San Costanzo 62
Procession of Sant' Antonio 62
Procida 72-76, **74**
  beaches 73
  directory 76
  entertainment 76
  festivals and events 76
  restaurants 75
  shopping 76
  transport 76
  what to do 76
  where to stay 75

R

rail travel 9
Ravello 38
Ravello Festival 17
Regata Storica delle Quattro Repubbliche Marinare 17
restaurants 13-16
  price codes 13
road travel 9, 10

S

safety 21
Sagra della Castagna 17
Sagra del Mare 76
Sagra del Pesce Azzurro 76
Sagra del Vino 76
sailing 70
Salerno 47
  entertainment 51
  restaurants 50
  shopping 51
  transport 51
  where to stay 50
Sant'Agata sui Due Golfi 28
Santa Maria del Soccorso 62
Sant'Angelo, Ischia 67
Sbarco dei Saraceni 17
Scala 36
sea travel 9, 12
Settembrata Anacaprese 17, 62
Settimana della Cultura 16
Sorrentine Peninsula 24-33
  directory 33
  entertainment 32
  restaurants 31
  shopping 32
  what to do 32
  where to stay 30
Sorrentine Peninsula and Amalfi Coast 23-51
  overview 6
Sorrento 25
  directory 33
  entertainment 32
  restaurants 31
  shopping 32
  transport 33
  what to do 32
  where to stay 30
Spiaggia di Marina Grande, Capri 57
Spiaggia Grande, Positano 35
Stabiae (Scavi di Stabia) 95
Suburban villas, Pompeii 94

T

telephone 21
tennis 33, 76
Tenuta Vannulo 49
Terme Stabiane, Pompeii 93
Terra Murata, Procida 73
Tiberius's Leap, Capri 56
tipping 21
Torca 28
Torre di Michelangelo, Ischia 65
tourist information 21
Trail of the Gods 28
trains 9
Tramonti 39
transport
  air 8
  airport information 8
  bicycle 11

car hire 11
rail 9
road 9, 10, 11
sea 9, 12

V

Valle dei Mulini 29
Vallone dei Mulini 26
Vesuvius 78-87
   directory 87
   entertainment 86
   restaurants 85
   transport 87
   what to do 86
   where to stay 85

Vesuvius, Herculaneum
   and Pompeii 77-98
   overview 6
Via del Mercurio,
   Pompeii 90
Vico Equense 25
Vietri 40
Villa Campolieto,
   Herculaneum 83
Villa Cimbrone, Ravello
   39
Villa dei Papiri,
   Herculaneum 82
Villa di Poppaea,
   Oplontis 95

Villa Jovis, Capri 56
Villa Rufolo, Ravello 39
Villa San Michele
   Anacapri 58
Ville Vesuviane,
   Herculaneum 83
voltage 22

W

walking 28, 33, 44, 55,
   59, 63, 70, 83,
   84, 87
where to stay 12-13
   price codes 13
wine 15-16, 44